There are numerous books to help parents through the sleepless nights and difficult days of infancy, the tumultuous terrible twos, the emotional roller coaster of puberty and the overall angst of adolescence. However, in my experience working with and studying parents, no period of their children's development is as perplexing for parents as emerging adulthood and no task more difficult than helping their children successfully transition to adulthood. Despite the challenges in and the importance of emerging adulthood, for no period of development have fewer books been written to help parents. That has changed completely with this book!

Varda Konstam provides parents with an empirically based book that delivers an insightful, informative, and interesting look into the major issues facing young people as they make the transition to adulthood. Konstam's experience as a teacher, clinician, researcher and parent enables her to present information and ideas in an accessible way that will empower parents to be able to help their children flourish rather than flounder as they navigate the wonderful yet perilous years of emerging adulthood.

—*Larry J. Nelson, PhD, Associate Professor,*
School of Family Life, Brigham Young University

Today parents and young adult children inhabit a new world of child-parent relationships. Konstam translates research findings on the worldview of today's young adults into sound parenting ideas. After a careful analysis of the economic and social transformations that place emerging adults in a world quite different from their parents' experience, Konstam helps parents think through the challenges of parenting in very pragmatic ways, with attention to issues in living together, finances, managing conflict and supporting the developing adult's full emergence.

Konstam's voice is clear, supportive and realistic. Throughout, she remains marvelously sympathetic and attuned to the perspectives of both parents and their emerging adults. This wise book helps parents understand their emerging adult children and provides an optimistic view of how parents can support the development of their children's adult identities.

—*Douglas Davies, MSW, PhD, Author of*
Child Development: A Practitioner's Guide, *Lecturer,*
School of Social Work, University of Michigan, Ann Arbor

PARENTING YOUR EMERGING ADULT

PARENTING YOUR EMERGING ADULT

Launching Kids from 18 to 29

DR. VARDA KONSTAM

New Horizon Press
Far Hills, New Jersey

To Marvin, Amanda, and Jeremy —
who continue to inspire me

Requests for permission should be addressed to:
New Horizon Press
P.O. Box 669
Far Hills, NJ 07931

Konstam, Varda
Parenting Your Emerging Adult: Launching Kids from 18 to 29

Cover design: Bob Aulicino
Interior design: Scribe Inc.

Library of Congress Control Number: 2012945206

ISBN-13: 978-0-88282-432-1
New Horizon Press

Manufactured in the U.S.A.

17   16   15   14   13   1   2   3   4   5

Author's Note

This book is based on the author's research, personal experience, interviews and life experiences.

The quest to define and reach adulthood plays itself out uniquely in every family. The voices of individuals used from the author's research come from different walks of life and different sociocultural contexts. In order to protect privacy, names have been changed and identifying characteristics have been altered except for contributing experts.

For purposes of simplifying usage, the pronouns his/her and s/he are sometimes used interchangeably. The information contained herein is not meant to be a substitute for professional evaluation and therapy with mental health professionals.

Acknowledgements

A special thank you to two exceptional individuals,
Selda Celen-Demirtas and Alex Bayne.

Their assistance, support and commitment
have been invaluable in writing this book
and have affirmed the best qualities
of this generation of emerging adults.

Contents

Chapter 1

"I CHILD-PROOFED MY HOUSE, BUT THEY STILL GET IN."

—Author unknown

In many ways more savvy and mature than their parents' generation, in other ways bewilderingly slow to develop, emerging adults are perplexing and hard to categorize as a group. They seem at once to be more fearless and yet more anxiety-ridden than generations past; more practical and yet more irresponsible, more globally aware and yet more self-absorbed, more interconnected and yet more isolated. The paradoxes persist.

Emerging adults are not a monolithic entity. Their behaviors are, in part, informed by the global, unpredictable and unstable context they are negotiating. In a world of lightning-fast social, technological and economic change, the future is a vast unknown for today's emerging adults. Familiarity, predictability and stability are in short supply. This generation of emerging adults may be the first generation that is growing up without the illusion that the world they will grow old in will look anything like the world they live in now. Ambiguity and uncertainty prevail.

Each generation, over the last century, has taken longer to assume the roles of adulthood than the previous one. Rather than viewing this as a problem to be fixed, it can also be viewed as a natural development, given that the world has grown vastly more complex and the fact that people live longer. The old rules no longer appear to apply. Being an emerging adult is a different experience today when compared to previous generations.

Who Are Emerging Adults and What Are They Thinking?

Dr. Jeffrey Arnett, a developmental psychologist, coined the term *emerging adulthood* to describe the stage of life that typically occurs between ages eighteen and twenty-nine years. It is interesting to note that, initially, emerging adulthood was thought to encompass ages eighteen to twenty-five. Recently, the age range was modified to reflect the way emerging adults are living their lives. Arnett's efforts have resulted in focused research efforts that are specific to this critical stage of development. In his ongoing work, Arnett explores the myths associated with emerging adulthood, myths that are often supported by the media and popular books.[1]

There is consensus among most developmental psychologists regarding what it means to be an emerging adult. Dr. Arnett identifies five features of emerging adulthood:

- Identity exploration
- Instability
- Self-focus
- Feeling in between
- Possibilities[2]

While it is a mistake to speak in one voice for an entire group, emerging adults share common concerns. Some of these are anxieties that previous generations did not face. Emerging adults today worry to an unprecedented degree about the state of the environment, the political and economic stability of the world and whether they will be able to protect the next generation—their children—from grievous harm and privation. Some emerging adults question whether it is responsible to have another generation of children.

Emerging adults worry about finding jobs that are suitable, match their skill sets and intellect and cover their living expenses. They are concerned about the wide array of problems they are inheriting but did nothing to create; problems neglected by their parents' generation, such as global environmental crises, dwindling natural resources, massive national debt, a broken Social Security system and spiraling healthcare and education costs.

Perhaps surprisingly, though, many emerging adults remain optimistic when it comes to their personal hopes and dreams. For the most part, they anticipate lives of success and fulfillment.[3] I believe they are in an intriguing place psychologically: They are aware of a larger, "perilous" world, yet at the same time they subscribe to a view of themselves as "empowered" and resilient, a stance that serves to buffer them against personal threat.[4] Across socioeconomic backgrounds, emerging adults tend to believe that they will prevail in life. However, "optimism frequently co-exists with an undercurrent of trepidation."[5] Many emerging adults feel anxious about the instability that surrounds them, but these anxious feelings are balanced by their sense of enthusiasm and optimism.

This is not, however, unique to emerging adults. Most individuals, regardless of age, tend to believe that unpleasant events will happen to others and not themselves. This belief in invincibility is a coping skill that helps individuals adapt to their environments. Adopting an optimistic outlook, even if it isn't entirely justifiable by the presenting facts, permits people to go forward with their lives and pursue their goals and dreams. It is easy to see why this coping style is particularly useful during emerging adulthood, a period in which a sense of instability pervades all things.

While most emerging adults remain hopeful about their own future lives, they are less optimistic and hopeful for the world in general in comparison to previous generations. The economic downturn from 2008 onward has given them ample reason to question the prevailing wisdom. However, it is important to note that most have not given up on the institutions of past generations.

Ambivalence is another key theme of emerging adulthood. Many young people are conflicted about entering adulthood.[6] They welcome the rights and responsibilities that accompany being an adult, including increased social status. However, they also associate adulthood with monotony, lack of spontaneity and the relinquishing of dreams. For many emerging adults, adulthood means replacing possibilities with major compromises. Arnett poses this question:

> Are they not right to recognize that adulthood, whatever its rewards, involves constraints and limitations that their lives during emerging adulthood do not have?…[It] seems evident that their ambivalence about adulthood is reasonable, and does not merit contempt or derision.[7]

Emerging adults are worried about taking the final step to adulthood, and with good reason. But a note of reassurance is in order: Few emerging adults actually fail to launch. By age thirty, "three-fourths have entered marriage and parenthood, nearly all have entered stable employment, nearly all have become financially independent and hardly any live with their parents."[8]

What Is Adulthood?

The search for a concrete definition of adulthood is difficult and elusive. There is no magical transition point that marks one's "arrival" as an adult. Typically, it is much easier to know when one is *not* in the presence of an adult. Chronological age provides only a crude approximation of maturity. Nevertheless, representative adults such as employers tend to view emerging adulthood with this invisible marker in mind.[9]

When and how do we know that emerging adults are *really* adults? How does an adult act and look different from an emerging adult? Adolescence, emerging adulthood and "full" adulthood lie on a continuum with no hard dividing lines. The exercise we will discuss next will help clarify and expand your own understanding. It was developed by Dr. Arnett.[10] As you work on this exercise, remember that your definition may differ from others in your network of friends and family. The aim of this exercise is for you to receive greater clarity in terms of your own definition.

Rate the importance of each of these criteria in terms of defining adulthood (1 indicates not at all important, 4 indicates very important).

Category	Criterion	Level of Importance
Role Transitions	Financially independent from parents	1 2 3 4
	No longer living in parents' household	1 2 3 4
	Finished education	1 2 3 4
	Married	1 2 3 4
	Has at least one child	1 2 3 4

Category	Criterion	Level of Importance			
Norm Compliance	Settled into a long-term career	1	2	3	4
	Purchased a house	1	2	3	4
	Avoids becoming drunk	1	2	3	4
	Avoids drunk driving	1	2	3	4
	Avoids illegal drugs	1	2	3	4
	Has no more than one sexual partner	1	2	3	4
	Avoids committing petty crimes like vandalism and shoplifting	1	2	3	4
	Drives safely and close to the speed limit	1	2	3	4
	Avoids use of profanity/ vulgar language	1	2	3	4
	Uses contraception if sexually active and not trying to conceive a child	1	2	3	4
Biological/Age Transitions	Reached age eighteen	1	2	3	4
	Reached age twenty-one	1	2	3	4
	Grown to full height	1	2	3	4
	If a woman, is biologically capable of bearing children	1	2	3	4
	If a man, is biologically capable of fathering children	1	2	3	4

Category	Criterion	Level of Importance			
	Has obtained license and can drive an automobile	1	2	3	4
	Has had sexual intercourse	1	2	3	4
	Is allowed to drink alcohol	1	2	3	4
	Is allowed to smoke cigarettes	1	2	3	4
Family Capacities	If a woman, is capable of supporting a family financially	1	2	3	4
	If a man, is capable of caring for children	1	2	3	4
	If a woman, is capable of caring for children	1	2	3	4
	If a man, is capable of running a household	1	2	3	4
	If a man, is capable of keeping family physically safe	1	2	3	4
	If a woman, is capable of keeping family physically safe	1	2	3	4
Relational Maturity	Accepts responsibility for consequences of actions	1	2	3	4
	Has relationship with parents as an equal adult	1	2	3	4
	Has good control of emotions	1	2	3	4
	Has become less self-oriented, developed greater consideration for others	1	2	3	4

Dr. Larry Nelson and his colleagues compared the criteria that parents endorsed with those that their unmarried emerging adults between eighteen and twenty-five years old stressed.[11] The emerging adults and their parents gave differing emphasis to many of the criteria, but they agreed on others.

Areas of agreement included: accepting responsibility for oneself, making independent decisions and becoming financially independent. In contrast to more traditional cultures, marriage was not viewed as a definitive marker of adulthood by emerging adults or parents. Both emerging adults and parents viewed relational maturity as highly significant when conferring adulthood status.

On the disagreement side, parents rated the Norm Compliance factors (e.g., avoids drunk driving, has no more than one sexual partner) as more important than their emerging adults did, while emerging adults gave Family Capacities greater weight.

Differences emerged not only between emerging adults and their parents, but also between mothers and fathers. Men and women varied in their emphases. For example, fathers assigned Norm Compliance factors greater importance than mothers did. Mothers, in contrast, assigned Relational Maturity factors higher values.

The gender of emerging adults and parents also influenced the results. Fathers in the sample rated Relational Maturity as more important when considering their sons versus their daughters. It may be that fathers view males as less competent in the domain of relational maturity and therefore rate those qualities more highly regarding their sons. Whatever the explanation, gender expectations are in play. Despite advances in gender equality, expectations still differ for emerging adult sons and daughters.

Emerging adult women considered Relational Maturity and Norm Compliance more important than emerging adult men did. These findings suggest that many parents socialize their daughters to become more care-oriented and may be more protective of them. The meaning of launching a child to adulthood differs for mothers and fathers, sons and daughters, parents and emerging adults. It is informed by cultural considerations.

How do your views regarding the status of adulthood differ when considering a male emerging adult versus a female? If there are differences, how do you feel about them? Is there anything that surprises you about your own attitudes? Are you projecting a double standard in any way? If so, do you feel this double standard is justified?

Defining Adulthood

When defining adulthood, is there any common ground? Attaining adulthood has a good deal to do with the ability to be responsible to oneself and others. Social and economic roles are important. The abilities to hold a job, sustain relationships and run an independent household suggest certain levels of freedom from parental dependence.

The definition of adulthood varies from culture to culture. In Chinese culture, for example, adulthood is associated with the ability to take care of one's parents. Adulthood in a consumer-driven society such as the United States is more likely to be associated with ownership of material goods.

Most emerging adults in the United States reject the idea that one is "complete" once one has entered adulthood. They prefer the view that adults continue to evolve and improve over a lifetime, revisiting and revising parts of the self. Emerging adults disapprove of stagnation and favor lifelong growth. They believe that reaching adulthood status is a gradual process that builds upon previous experience and that it does not necessarily occur in all dimensions of their lives simultaneously. Physical maturity, emotional maturity and artistic maturity, for example, may occur at very different ages.

Regardless of gender and generation, there does appear to be a consensus regarding entry to adulthood:

- Accepting responsibility for oneself and one's actions
- Making independent decisions
- Becoming financially independent[12]

These criteria are viewed as gradual and incremental rather than all-or-nothing. Emerging adults do not tend to view marital status as key to attaining adulthood status.[13]

Additional Factors

Adulthood is an opportunity to negotiate differences and to learn about what one wants and doesn't want. In the process, emerging adults can discover that they are no longer dependent on the whims of others and can respond in ways that are consistent with their own values and identities. According to Dr. Harry Blatterer, author of *Coming of Age in Times of Uncertainty*, adulthood brings an increasing sense that despite supports, one ultimately has to be responsible for oneself and take a proactive stance in relation to one's future.[14]

Dr. Blatterer offers added observations about the meaning of adulthood. He notes that some of the new freedoms of adulthood may carry a price tag: a newfound sense of isolation. One emerging adult expressed that "adult" feeling this way: "No one is gonna look after me. I have to look after myself; I'm an independent and discrete person."

Adulthood includes the acceptance of one's aloneness, despite how scary it may feel.[15]

Loss of innocence is another milestone that marks the transition to adulthood. The realization that power, politics and appearances, as opposed to substance, justice, talent and fairness, often play major roles in the adult world can be disillusioning.[16] The emerging adult relinquishes a notion of the world as he or she imagined it to be and comes to terms with the world as it is. However, this does not necessarily mean that one forfeits belief in the possibility of a better world. One can experience the loss of innocence and still strive to make the world better.

The presidential campaigns of Hillary Clinton and Barack Obama, candidates in the 2008 United States presidential election, in some ways exemplified this tension. Barack Obama boldly stated that "yes we can" hope and dream, while Hillary Clinton retorted that he was living in a "fairy tale." The Clinton campaign's model of adulthood implied giving up fairy tales and favoring practical realities. Many emerging adults (who voted overwhelmingly for President Obama) are reassessing but still believe in the dream.

Another characteristic of adulthood is the ability to mold oneself to social expectations other than those of one's family.[17] This is a challenge given that children, adolescents and emerging adults in recent decades have been taught to value *authenticity*, the idea of being true and real to themselves. As they mature, they perceive that in many settings, such as the workplace, they are asked to be *in*authentic. This creates inner conflict. Grappling with the issue of authenticity versus artificial role-playing means leaving an idealized world and coming to terms with what is. This is a developmental task that many emerging adults have a difficult time with, given the importance of authenticity in their lives. Learning how to assume social roles while retaining one's authenticity seems to be an important hallmark of modern adulthood.

The next section provides us with an opportunity to observe Caroline, an emerging adult, and her mother, Alicia Reardon, who help illustrate some of the tensions that can exist between emerging adults and their parents. These tensions are in part due to different world views regarding what an emerging adult is and is not.

Caroline and Alicia Reardon

Caroline and Alicia, a divorced single mother, find themselves arguing over who is in charge of Caroline's life. Caroline is an articulate twenty-six-year-old who has recently moved out of her mother's home. Caroline and her mother view the world very differently and have distinct ideas about how Caroline's twenties should unfold. Both Caroline and her mother are entrenched in their respective positions. The tensions between them are substantial and are having a negative effect on other members of the family, a younger sister and brother.

As you read these accounts, think about these questions: Can you empathize with Caroline's perspective on adulthood or do you view her as coddled and entitled? If you were a friend of Alicia's, how would you respond to the tensions she describes?

Caroline's Perspective

My twenty-seventh birthday is a week away and I thought I would be an adult by now. I have a solid job. I'm in graduate school. I live on my own and I pay my own bills. When will it be enough for my mother to get off my back when I want to go on vacation? It's my choice what I do with my vacation time and my earned money! I think that if I can pay my own bills with no issues, then I should be able to do what I want to do.

I want to go to Iceland for a week with my friends. My mother is giving me a hard time about it and it is just not fair. When do I get to have fun again like when I was an undergraduate? I work a sixty-hour-a-week job and I'm barely getting enough sleep. If I want a week to chill, THEN I WILL.

Every time I try to plan something just for me, my mother tells me I'm not acting like the adult I am. To that I say, if I am an adult then it shouldn't matter what I do and she should lay off! I know she only says that kind of stuff because by my age she was married with kids and didn't have the time or money to do anything. She worries about me spending my money frivolously, and I know that it is tied to her childhood and not having a lot of money. She worries about me getting into a bind and then what am I going to do? She thinks I'll go straight to her and my father.

She doesn't know I've already bought the airplane tickets to Iceland with my student loan money. I'm going to tell her that I'm visiting a friend in San Francisco and my cell phone battery just happened to die on the trip.

I am going to be twenty-seven years old and I'm still lying to my parent! When am I going to be an adult?

Alicia's Perspective

I worry so much about Caroline. She doesn't understand that bills do not just stop when you go on vacation. Employers don't let you just leave for weeks at a time. She hasn't lasted more than two years at a job. I've been at my job for twenty years! I just want her to put money in her account for a rainy day, so then maybe I can finally retire and stop bailing her out of her problems. She wanted to move out of the house on her own and didn't have the collateral, so who gave her the money? I did.

She needs to learn that being an adult is not just about making decisions. It is about making the right decisions; the right decisions for your family.

That's another thing. When is she going to settle down? She has to become an adult. What if she gets fired? What is she going to tell her landlord? "Sorry, sir, I went to Iceland and so I can't pay my rent this month. Can I owe you the money?" She'll end up back in my house and I just cannot let her fail like that. I think I need to keep pushing her to be more responsible. I'm not going to be here forever to bail her out. I worry so much about her. She just does not "get it."

Caroline and Alicia view Caroline's life from different perspectives. Caroline is stuck in a rebellious, dependent and sometimes hostile stance. She disregards her mother's appeals to act more responsibly. Caroline resents her mother's judgments but does not seem to recognize that these judgments no longer have any real power in her adult life.

Alicia is locked in a nagging pattern guided by the belief that she "cannot let Caroline fail." It is difficult for her to relinquish control. This stance ensures continuing tensions between Alicia and her daughter. To complicate matters further, she is concerned that Caroline will mimic her father's irresponsible money management behavior. Alicia is coming from a position of fear, which seldom produces positive change. She engages with

Caroline in a self-defeating dance, leaving little space for the possibility for different dance steps to emerge.

Who is in charge of Caroline and her life? What can Caroline do? What can Alicia do to improve their relationship? We will revisit the Reardons in chapter 9 and take a closer look at how they might change their "dance" to a new one.

In this book I address key issues related to the developmental period of emerging adulthood. We will immerse ourselves in the experiences and diverse perspectives of emerging adults trying to negotiate environments characterized by complexity and uncertainty. After reviewing the opinions of other experts and their research, as well as my own research and clinical experiences, we'll look at emerging adults and their parents trying to navigate the best they can with the tools they have. You will be asked to consider the complexity of the presenting issues and you will learn strategies and techniques for becoming more adept at identifying the relevant questions and proposing possible solutions.

As you learn more about the theories and issues you will also become increasingly skillful at integrating the two and applying them to situations with your emerging adult. This book will not provide you with all the answers, but it *will* endeavor to give you a better understanding of the challenges emerging adults and their parents encounter and how better to navigate them. The challenges we will discuss are everyday challenges that fall within the norm. This book will not address emerging adult issues that are more serious in scope, such as intransigent emotional problems that require ongoing psychiatric intervention. In the process, I believe you will gain an increased understanding of the complex terrain people eighteen to twenty-nine years of age are navigating as well as increased appreciation and empathy for your emerging adult.

Simplistic depictions of this generation of emerging adults are not, in my opinion, beneficial. This new generation defies easy characterizations. To dismiss them as immature and self-focused does not acknowledge the realities, costs and benefits associated with becoming an adult in the twenty-first century. Financially, for example, it is more difficult to strike out on one's own. A minimum-wage or entry-level job doesn't cover the expenses of independent living, especially when a young man or woman must repay massive student loans.

I feel we need to be more self-reflective before passing judgment on emerging adults or trying to shoehorn them into careers and lifestyles more typical of previous generations. Emerging adults have seen many of the mistakes their parents have made and are not eager to repeat them. They grew up in a world in which half of all marriages ended in divorce. They have watched many of their parents give their allegiance to sixty- or seventy-hour-a-week jobs, only to be "downsized" from their corporate offices. They have seen our planet's resources diminish frighteningly as a consumer culture preached material success as the main criterion of a life well-lived. They don't want to repeat their parents' mistakes; they want to do better. They have to figure it out themselves.

How can we do this? Where can we turn for answers? Bill O'Hanlon, a solution-focused therapist and prolific author, tells a funny story along these lines.[18] An instructor, who is unmarried with no children, teaches a popular course titled "Ten Commandments for Parents." He eventually meets the woman of his dreams, marries and has a child. After experiencing life as a parent, he re-titles his course: "Five Suggestions for Parents." More time passes and he becomes the proud parent of a second child. He soon finds himself renaming the course again: "Three Tentative

Hints for Parents." After his third child, he stops teaching the class altogether.[19]

In this book we will concentrate on understanding emerging adults and the issues that may surface for professionals working with them across diverse contexts. I hope to help you integrate what we know to date and discuss things I've learned from actively listening to a wide array of emerging adults, parents and employers—the major "stakeholders"—speak about this developmental period.

Chapter 2

EMERGING ADULTS AT WORK

Coddled, self-indulgent and undisciplined? Or savvy, prudent, yet experimental? Characterizations of today's emerging adults vary significantly. One popular view is that this generation is the most pampered in history, owing perhaps to the fact that their parents chose them more deliberately than any generation in the past. As a result, this generation of emerging adults has received too much attention. Another view portrays emerging adults as the screwed generation, having been utterly failed by a system that has not invested enough in their futures.[1]

So which is it? Have we lavished too much attention on our children or not enough? Again, when speaking about a generation this wide and deep, competing views are bound to emerge. In my opinion, there is truth to both sides of the argument. And both sides offer insights into the way emerging adults are approaching the workplace today.

This chapter focuses on the experiences of emerging adults at work, including their expectations and frustrations with the disconnect they are feeling in terms of what they thought the world of work would be like and what they are encountering.

As parents, you are undoubtedly witnessing some of the struggles your children are facing. Many emerging adults feel burdened by the realization that it may be up to them to "clean up the mess" that previous generations have created. This is coloring the way they view career, work and social responsibility. They are wary. They don't want to play the game the same way their parents played it. They are hesitant to buy into old rules. They do not plan to jump in with blinders on. They want to know what they are getting in return.

There are other major factors at play. Much of the world has recently experienced an economic downturn of significant proportions. This, too, has had a dramatic impact on the lives of emerging adults trying to enter the job market and build their careers. Institutions are breaking down; the rules of business are changing faster; promises made to new generations are being broken.

It is a confusing and disheartening picture.

What do emerging adults have to say about their work lives? We'll look at extensive interviews with emerging adults. We will listen to them speak about the challenges of today's workplace. I will also offer comments and insights based on my research and experience with emerging adults. Throughout, I ask you to consider these questions: If you were an emerging adult during such changing and uncertain times, how would you chart your course? How would it be different from the course you navigated back in your twenties?

Emerging adults today are getting on the career track more slowly and with more setbacks than previous generations did. It is easy to blame them and assume that since they are not "playing the game" the way past generations did, they are bringing their problems on themselves. But this, I think, is an unexamined view. The career world of today is vastly different from the world previous generations faced in their twenties. And yet schools, families and media pundits seem to be clinging to the old rules and expectations. No one has rewritten the handbook of working life to reflect today's realities. Given that, how could emerging adults feel anything but confused? They are being told to do one thing, yet the world is rewarding something quite different.

A New Orientation

When we look at several factors—including the uncertain state of the economy and the changes in corporate America and other countries in recent decades—we can understand why the new generation may be frustrated and angry.

However, it is important to note that although the terrain may be shifting, emerging adults overwhelmingly aspire toward traditional goals. They seem to want the same basic things their parents want for them: a satisfying career, marriage or a committed relationship and children. But they are trying to achieve these goals in their own way. This generation of emerging adults places emphasis on experimentation and personal choice. And why wouldn't they? The old paradigms have collapsed. Let's consider underlying principles and assumptions that fueled career decisions only a few decades ago:

- Be loyal to the company and it will be loyal to you.

- Work hard and you will be able to climb the corporate ladder, one rung at a time.

- Put in your years faithfully and you can count on a secure retirement.

- The economy will always be growing; there will always be good jobs for those who want them.

- Do a good job and be conscientious; you will be rewarded with a stable career.

- America is the world leader in most industries. Join an established American company and you cannot go wrong.

- A good education is the key to a good career.

- Certain careers, such as medicine, will always be stable and rewarding.

- A good job comes with good benefits, such as health insurance.

- Your pension will be there to support you when you retire.

- Your income, prestige and buying power will increase the older you get and the longer you work.

- If you are willing to trade off a little upper-end income potential, lifetime job security can be yours.

All of these promises have been broken or disappeared, yet we don't seem to have created any new and reliable promises to replace them. Given this, it makes perfect sense for emerging adults to be more experimental in their careers and to rely more on personal experience than on traditional corporate party lines. But because of this new orientation, it is taking the current generation quite a bit longer to put it all together.

The economic downturn, coupled with the recent seismic changes in industry, is doing nothing to help. Current work conditions are causing a huge disconnect between the world many emerging adults envisioned as they were pursuing an education and the world they are encountering in reality. Their fundamental belief that one ought not to "settle" for a job that is less than what one truly desires is being challenged at its core. Tensions are abundant. This is not the career world for which emerging adults signed up!

A large number of emerging adults remain committed to finding the "right" career and the "right" person, very frequently in that order. However, the economy is wreaking havoc with their plans. The rungs on the corporate ladder have either vanished or are being occupied by those ahead of them in the workforce.[2]

Emerging adults are having trouble attaining entry-level jobs because those are being held by people in their thirties. Thirty-somethings, who had expected to be in management by now, find higher career rungs blocked by older Gen Xers. And forty-somethings can no longer move into the executive ranks because those rungs are still inhabited by Boomers who were supposed to have retired by now! The corporate ladder, to the extent it even exists any longer, is jammed up.

Due to a complex of reasons— among them slower maturation, longer educational paths, a clogged corporate ladder and a significant downturn in interdependent economies worldwide— many emerging adults are not moving rapidly into stable careers. On average, they are taking about five to ten years longer to cement their work and personal lives than the Boomer generation.[3] This is particularly true of those who come from backgrounds of relative affluence.

Understandably, this delay may be triggering concerns for you, the parent. Is this generation—and your son or daughter in particular—ever going to "settle down"? Remember, though, the encouraging news I shared in chapter 1: by approximately age thirty, most emerging adults do manage to establish careers.[4] It is more a question of *when* than *if*, though it may not always seem that way to you.

Shattered Expectations

When you are dealing with your emerging adult on career issues, it is helpful to keep in mind the vast change in expectations with which emerging adults are grappling. Their loss of innocence as they enter the workforce is on a scale far greater than ever before.[5]

Most emerging adults enter their twenties with high hopes. Upon graduating from college, they find themselves encountering shocks that are difficult to digest. The job market they see is one characterized by impermanence, insecurity and lack of structural supports. Not only have there been profound changes in the *types* of jobs that are available, but in the *number* as well. The steep economic downturn has resulted in alarming unemployment rates and massive cutbacks. The ratio of available positions to qualified candidates has shrunk precipitously. Each job opening generates hundreds if not thousands of résumé submissions. As noted by Jean Twenge, a social psychologist at San Diego University, many emerging adults are feeling disillusioned and betrayed. Well-paying jobs with promising career trajectories are rare. Being an upstanding member of the middle class is becoming increasingly challenging.[6]

These realities are particularly difficult for today's emerging adults to accept, given that they are better educated, enjoy more modern conveniences and have access to more goods and services than any previous generation. They are accustomed to a relatively high standard of living and are shocked to find themselves unable to maintain it for themselves, even when they have "good" jobs. The world, they feel, has made them promises that it is now unable to keep. Many emerging adults are struggling with deep disillusionment and anxiety about the future.

Emerging adults did not anticipate the disconnect they are experiencing between the world that was promised them and the real world they are facing. Long-held assumptions are being shattered on every front. Our emerging adults feel "gypped," as one parent I interviewed noted. The path to adulthood can be a quagmire even in the best of times. But when today's career uncertainty is added to the mix, it creates a serious new threat to their senses of safety and security.

Emerging adults are handling this "crisis" in various ways. Some internalize their disappointments, blame themselves and feel anxious and/or depressed. Others become angry at the system that has failed them, due to what they see as gross negligence on the part of their elders. Those who feel the most threatened are workers in entry-level jobs that require no specific skill sets other than perhaps a college degree and offer no clear path toward advancement. Those who choose highly differentiated fields such as medicine, engineering or fields with specific and valued skill sets are less likely to express these concerns. Still, even formerly enduring careers such as medicine are proving more and more financially challenging.

Emerging adults feel that they are on their own, navigating uncharted territory without a compass and without any support from society. From their perspective, there is little or no assurance that their contributions will be acknowledged or appreciated. They are being told that they are fortunate to have jobs (for those who have found jobs), but they also feel stuck and discouraged. It is not surprising that in many cases they are reaching out to parents to supply the emotional support and expertise that they need.

Loyalty

Loyalty in the workplace is a prime issue on the minds of many emerging adults. Traditionally loyalty has been touted as one of the key qualities an employee brings to the job. The unwritten rule, for past generations, was *be loyal to the company and the company will be loyal to you.* But today's emerging adults have seen that contract shattered as the workforce has become commoditized and dispensable. In today's highly competitive, fluid labor market, emerging adults are keenly aware of the eroding trust among employers, employees and the institutions they serve. Many have witnessed the devastating effects of "downsizing" and "restructuring" in their own parents' lives. They have repeatedly seen loyal, long-term employees unceremoniously terminated.

Many firms no longer reward employee loyalty with job security and opportunity, yet the expectations have not really changed for the employees.[7] Corporations still expect loyalty from them, even as corporations have demonstrated that they have neither the means nor the intent to repay that loyalty. Emerging adults are wrestling with how to handle that contradiction.

Emerging adults are determined not to replicate their parents' experiences. They do not intend to give years of blind loyalty to a job in exchange for flimsy and empty promises. Feeling responsible only to themselves, they are trying to minimize their vulnerability and disposability by actively managing their own careers, a plan that often runs aground in today's economic climate. Many emerging adults have tried to learn skill sets that they thought would better position them for their next opportunities. However, they are finding that it is hard to be mobile when the jobs just aren't there. Thus they find themselves stuck between an old "stay loyal to the company" model that no longer works and a new "manage your own career" model that can't gain any traction.

Additionally, they are blamed for their slow career movement. Many emerging adults are realizing that there are few opportunities for professional mentoring in today's career world. A common perception is that emerging adult employees are viewed as resources to be exploited by their employers. As a result, they feel compelled to look out for themselves, to be their own mentors. There seems to be a vicious cycle at play here: Companies are growing more and more reluctant to invest their resources in grooming employees who might wish to leave in one to two years (taking their freshly-groomed skills to the competition if the marketplace permits them the opportunity to do so). Meanwhile, emerging adults are trying to leave jobs due to that lack of career development opportunity.

Thus we see a nomadic lifestyle in which many emerging adults are moving, somewhat aimlessly, in search of opportunity. Given the feeling that the marketplace views them as disposable commodities, emerging adults have taken to believing that they have to fend for themselves. Changing jobs frequently is associated with building skill sets and positioning themselves to thrive in a challenging market.

It is often the quest for passion and fulfillment that guides their search. Many in this generation of emerging adults don't want to settle for jobs they merely *can* do; they want to find work in which they can make a meaningful contribution and derive a sense of true satisfaction. Yet the economic realities are forcing many emerging adults to put passion on hold. This is creating what I call "the passion dilemma."

The Passion Dilemma

Before the worldwide economic downturn, *passion* was the buzzword for many emerging adults. Their expectations for themselves and their careers were high, perhaps at an all-time high. This generation of emerging adults was raised to "follow your bliss" and it learned its lessons well: work was supposed to be meaningful, engaging and fun. Some even expected it to be exhilarating.

Motivated in part by the desire not to replicate their parents' experiences and in part by the optimistic messaging on which they were raised, their plan was to seek jobs that offered fulfillment, challenge and meaning. As a nice side benefit, they also thought they would be financially rewarded for their efforts. For many emerging adults, the pursuit of fulfillment in the job market is proving to be both elusive and illusory. As a result, they are becoming anxious and despondent about future prospects.

Emerging adults assume a diversity of approaches in trying to choose a career. While some may pursue paths that are linear and prescribed without prior reflection about their values and attitudes, others engage in experimentation, changing jobs every year or two (or whenever possible), in an attempt to find their passions. Still others pursue careers without considering their unique skills and how they may fit in with the current marketplace. Finding one's passion at work is viewed by many emerging adults as the key to self-fulfillment, yet jobs that meet this high expectation are in short supply. There is an assumption on the part of many emerging adults that there exists a "right" job. It is their responsibility to figure out what their "right" jobs are and these decisions should be informed by passion.

The experiences of emerging adults in the workplace may raise questions for you in your role as parent. What are your views about passion?

- Do you consider being passionate about one's work necessary for fulfillment and happiness?

- What messages did you give your child about passion and career when your son or daughter was growing up?

Would you revise those messages now if you had the chance?

- What kind of model have you provided for your emerging adult? Have you pursued passion in your own career? Have you encouraged your emerging adult to follow your modeling or have you told him or her not to make the same mistakes you made?

- How do you feel about the pursuit of passion in the workplace? Is it wise and appropriate? Should it be a primary pursuit or a secondary one? Are security and salary more important?

- Do you believe in the maxim, "Do what you love and the money will follow"?

- Do you have spiritual beliefs about finding one's purpose in life? Do you believe that each of us is "designed" to do one thing better than anyone else? Do you use words such as *calling* and *destiny*?

- Do you see career as the center of one's life or as merely one important aspect among many?

- If your emerging adult is not able to find passion at work, does it imply a deficiency, a life that is "less than"?

- Have you ever seen your emerging adult engaged in activities that put him or her "in the zone" or in a state of "flow"? Is he or she incorporating any of these activities in her career life? Do you think he or she should be? Why?

- Do you and your emerging adult differ in your opinions about the importance of passion and does it create tensions in your relationship?

Passion and the pursuit of the perfect job/perfect life tend to be intertwined for emerging adults (and many of their parents). Christine Hassler, in her book *20-Something, 20-Everything: A Quarter-Life Woman's Guide to Balance and Direction*, provides an illuminating discussion of passion and how it is often viewed as the basis for measuring work success.[8] She suggests that most emerging adults are not particularly good at identifying their passions. Also, passion means different things to different people. For Hassler it implies a "fire burning in our bellies" that will drive people toward career fulfillment and well-being. But she suggests that the search for passion may leave some feeling vulnerable and despondent: "…we have become obsessed with finding our passions, and a lot of us have found suffering instead."[9]

For many emerging adults, finding purpose and passion at work is an elusive process. It leads to a yearning for the perfect job, a yearning that places tremendous pressure on emerging adults. Could it be that young men and women are asking too much of their jobs? Could it be that they are looking too hard for fulfillment in that single area of their lives? Perhaps by putting so much pressure on themselves to find passion in the workplace they are shutting off the flow of the very passion they are seeking.

How do you feel about the passion dilemma? How does it affect you in the role of parent? What if your emerging adult is unable to identify his or her passion?

Distributing the Passion

Work has taken center stage for many emerging adults and their parents. The job one does for a living has been given larger-than-life meaning at the expense of other important domains of life. How did this come about? Perhaps it has been a response to uncertain times; perhaps it represents people's attempt to take control of their lives and the lives of their children. Today, both men and women feel driven to seek their fulfillment in the workplace. The sense of balance for some has been lost. Now many define their identities by what they do for a paycheck.

Paradoxically, such an approach may leave emerging adults feeling *more* vulnerable in the long run, especially when the economy doggedly insists on showing them that they are not in control. As Hassler suggests, psychologically, it is better to separate what one does from who one is, otherwise one remains vulnerable to the whims of industry and the economy.[10] People's identities could be wiped out by a simple shift in the job market. Additionally, as Hassler notes, "No job can fill a void or complete us."[11] Passion should not come from one place alone.

A partial solution to the passion dilemma might lie in spreading the passion around. Perhaps we need to encourage today's emerging adults to work harder at seeking passion from and infusing passion *into* other areas of their lives. This is especially true during times when the job market is a passion drought.

Dr. John L. Holland, a well-regarded leader in the field of career counseling, suggests that there may not be enough jobs in the future to satisfy special interests.[12] He further suggests that it is probably unrealistic to expect a single job to satisfy all of one's needs or to reflect all of the aspects of one's personality. That means people need to look toward other aspects of their lives, such as hobbies, lifestyles, communities and relationships, to find a sense of satisfaction. This change in emphasis will be a very positive thing. By recognizing the inherent limitations of jobs in providing total fulfillment, emerging adults will naturally give more attention to other domains of life. And in so doing, they will become happier, more fully rounded adults.

A recent study I completed with my colleague Dr. Ilana Lehmann (of 486 emerging adults twenty-five to thirty years of age) provides a window to understanding the important role of leisure in our lives.[13] We found that emerging adults were less likely to be indecisive about their careers if they enjoyed a satisfying leisure life. Having a fulfilling life outside of work seems to be additive and enriching and is associated with an increased likelihood of having clarity in career choice.

As we encourage our emerging adults to live passionately and fully, it seems inevitable that we, as a society, need to reexamine the central role of work in our lives. Even if the economy rebounds well and produces a surplus of exciting and stimulating jobs, we might want to rethink the amount of emphasis we have given to work when it comes to defining our happiness. Our play time, rest time, volunteering time and relationship time can provide at least as much passion and satisfaction as our job time. As Mark Twain astutely observed, "Work and play are words used to describe the same thing under differing conditions."[14]

Even the term *passion* itself may be putting unnecessary pressure on emerging adults. The implication is that we all have the "fire burning in our bellies" about which Hassler talks and that people only need to expose themselves to the right job situations in order to discover it. Passion suggests heat, intensity, lust and hunger. But maybe this isn't the way it works for everyone. Maybe some people don't feel their "callings" in life as burning passion. For some, perhaps it is only the gentlest of pulls, the faintest of whispers. And maybe that's okay. Maybe telling everyone to find a passion is a misleading notion.

I suggest a low-pressure route to the pursuit of happiness, an alternative way of framing the search. Perhaps what emerging adults need to look for in their jobs are a few elements that they value and enjoy. Think about the activities that your emerging adult enjoys so much that she or he gets lost in them and loses track of time. Think about the principles, topics and ideas your emerging adult values. Maybe finding a job that incorporates both of these elements is "good enough."

Perhaps identifying and pursuing a few job requirements may be a more manageable goal for your son or daughter than trying to unlock his or her hidden life passion. The pressure on your emerging adult and you may ease significantly as a result. For example, your emerging adult's dream job may entail working outdoors with other people in a company that is environmentally responsible. Instead of searching for her *passion*, your emerging adult might pursue a job that incorporates the elements that she values and enjoys. In the process, she might experience a good deal of fulfillment and gratification. Later, if passion arises, all the better.

More Suggestions and Insights to Consider

Perhaps today's emerging adults, by entering the workforce at such an uncertain time, will be forever marked by a sense of privation and frugality, as many who came of age during the Great Depression were. Or maybe they will become more like Gen Xers who entered the workplace in the recessionary nineties, during a time of massive cutbacks. The result: They became plucky, self-reliant career managers. Most emerging adults I interviewed were savvy and resilient. A substantial minority, though, were overwhelmed by the changing tide and felt disillusioned and despondent.

Jessica Godofsky, Cliff Zukin and Carl Van Horn, researchers at the John J. Heldrich Center for Workforce Development, found interesting results when they asked recent college graduates what they would do differently if they had a chance to live their college experiences all over again.[15] Many college graduates said that they would be more careful and thoughtful about the process of choosing a major and would select different majors, ones that would presumably lead to a greater number of job opportunities than they encountered. They also stated they would elect to do more internships and/or work part-time during college as well as start their searches for full-time jobs while still in college. Finally, they would take more classes to prepare them for careers. Their advice suggests endorsement of a more deliberate approach to linking college courses and experiences to potential employment opportunities.

As you try to support your son or daughter in forging a fulfilling career, it may be necessary to rethink the entire paradigm society has been using. Perhaps the whole idea of *finding* a dream job that will provide fulfillment is outmoded. Maybe the new paradigm will involve *creating* that dream job. There is ample, mounting evidence that corporations and big business will not hold the same promise for new generations that they held for previous ones. The promise of tomorrow may lie, instead, with becoming entrepreneurial. Individuals in all professions may soon need to become more entrepreneurial in order to survive.

With each passing year, more of the world provides the most abundant, best and least expensive goods and services. For instance, China and Japan manufacture much of the world's electronics. India writes software and provides technical support. This trend is unlikely to change any time soon. This can be good news or bad news depending upon how one reacts to it. One can use the new economic climate to one's advantage.

Any product or service that can be commoditized will eventually be commoditized, many at a cheaper rate than we can accomplish in the United States. So where does that leave our emerging adults?

I feel that innovation and creative thinking will serve them well. The secret to succeeding, now and in the future, may be to perform a very specific role or offer a very specific product or service in a fresh, personal and unique way, a way that no one else is doing. The customer base may be relatively small and specialized, but, with the entire world as one's market, that may well be enough to allow an emerging adult to thrive.

There is currently a disconnect between the skill sets that emerging adults are bringing to the marketplace and existing jobs. It is not, as commonly perceived, an issue of lack of availability of jobs but rather that the jobs that are available are not in synch with educational experiences and skill sets. One possible solution involves a paradigm shift. Emerging adults can be encouraged to learn how to become entrepreneurs, if so inclined, and start to grow their own businesses and generate new jobs for themselves as well as for others. Presently, for those emerging adults who are likely to embrace this underdeveloped area, possibilities for entrepreneurship training are in short supply.[16]

Emerging adults are in need of new skills to become engaged with the global marketplace. In an article appearing in *The American*, Arnold Kling and Nick Schultz point to inherent structural problems that are disabling the American economy.[17] Most of the jobs lost to the economic downturn are not coming back, in large part due to advances that are being made in new technologies and businesses. Fewer employees are needed because of gains in productivity that are associated with these advances. According to Kling and Schultz, bottom-up innovation is sorely needed. Existing top-down command and control practices in dominant industries such as education and healthcare are inefficient. They are not well situated to disrupt ineffective practices.

In many ways emerging adults are optimally positioned to take on this pressing need. They tend to embrace experimentation

and are apt to seek experiences that align with their perceived in-
tellectual capacities; however, they need the skill sets that allow
them to disrupt existing practices and solve long-term structural
problems. The promotion of entrepreneurship education is critical in terms of addressing the economic difficulties the economy
is currently encountering.

So, perhaps it does circle back to passion after all. Maybe
it is through discovering one's passion and uniqueness that one
discovers one's marketing edge in the new world.

Your emerging adult should be thinking more like a small
businessperson and less like an employee. Looking to major corporations for one's future security no longer offers guarantees.
Your emerging adult's intuitive sense that fending for him or herself is necessary should be encouraged. Even during those periods
when your emerging adult is working on salary for a big company, thinking of being in a small business that is contracting its
services to a single buyer may well be adaptive. Your emerging
adult should be using that opportunity to develop skills in a
uniquely tailored way. By doing one thing well, developing a reputation for it and eventually generating effective publicity for it,
your emerging adult will probably fare much better than she or
he would by endlessly searching for the perfect "fit" with existing
jobs in the workplace. In the new world, it is those who rise above
the landscape who are noticed. Encourage your emerging adults
to be proactive, creative and entrepreneurial with their careers.
That may be what it takes to both survive and thrive in the near
future.

Chapter 3

CAREER INDECISION OR EXPERIMENTATION?

You have seen the pattern, maybe in your own home. Many emerging adults may be changing jobs frequently, some every year or two, often without apparent career advancement. Or they are unemployed or *under*employed for periods that may stretch on for years. A growing number of emerging adults report feeling unfocused, "lost" and in a place they describe as "nowhere."[1] They fear they won't be able to find a satisfying career identity. As a result, many become reluctant to choose at all.[2]

What if your emerging adult seems confused and/or stuck and unable to decide on a career? You may be perplexed by your emerging adult's apparent indecisiveness and feeling as though your son or daughter should just make a decision and commit! At the same time, you may also recognize that your emerging adult is likely to have many careers over his or her lifespan and that the process of establishing a career is just that: a process.

Let's turn our attention to issues related to your emerging adult's career indecision, specifically how it is different from career experimentation, and explore possible solutions. We are going to focus now on how you can reach a better understanding about what may be going on in your son's or daughter's career decision-making process. We'll discuss insights and information to assist you in helping your undecided emerging adult to move forward more quickly.

No Easy Answers

Do you know any men or women in their mid or late thirties who are committed to promising careers? What was the process like for them? My guess is that in their mid-twenties many of them had not yet identified a firm career path. They had difficulties finding jobs and they probably had many job experiences, some of which seemed totally unrelated to one another. They zigzagged their way to a clearer choice.

The twenties often are a zigzagging decade. Those in that age range are likely to be unfocused and unsettled. What does that mean for parents? Be optimistic and realize that this is not necessarily a permanent condition. What looks like random indecision may make sense in hindsight, if not right now. My experience counseling emerging adults has made me more sensitive to the fact that their process of career selection is likely to be *nonlinear*. Try not to expect straight lines and neat "B follows A" progressions. The decision to keep one's career choice open well into one's twenties, for example, may be a wise choice for some. After all, emerging adults develop at different rates and selecting a career has become increasingly complex.

Then how do parents figure out what is healthy and what is not? When is an emerging adult's career "wandering" a wise response to a fluid job market and when does it become a problem that needs addressing? When are parents witnessing a healthy exercise in self-discovery and when are they seeing fear and avoidance? In the latter cases, what should parents do about these issues? Once again, there are no easy answers.

Professionals in the field are asking the same questions you are asking as a parent and finding that they must search hard for answers that can be elusive. Do not lose hope. Probing more deeply into the issues may bring more clarity about how to help emerging adults facing career decisions.

Not all career "wandering" or "stuckness" is a result of indecision, nor is it necessarily a sign of trouble. Career counselors have two different terms to capture career indecisiveness among emerging adults. One is a normative phase in career development which is referred to as *developmental indecision*. It occurs before the emerging adult makes a career choice. It is characterized as temporary and associated with resolution.[3]

In contrast to developmental indecision, *career indecision* is viewed as chronic and pervasive. Career indecision is defined as "involving the difficulties encountered by individuals in making career decision."[4] It is an all-encompassing term that refers to the range of difficulties individuals encounter in the decision-making process.

How do we distinguish emerging adults who are having genuine problems with career choice (floundering) from those who are experimenting? In many ways, they may look the same, at least in snapshot view. They both may *seem* to be wandering aimlessly and making choices that defy wisdom. Yet, while those who are experimenting might appear to be acting in an unfocused and random way, they may be successfully forging career identities. Flounderers are in need of guidance. Sadly, there is little research to enlighten us on "floundering," even though the implications of this growing phenomenon may be huge to our society.

According to the United States Department of Labor, of the jobs held by eighteen to twenty-four-year-old workers, 56 percent ended in one year or less and another 14 percent ended in under two years.[5] Many of today's emerging adults are taking a "sampling" approach to the job menu. A lot of this has to do with the exploration of identity that naturally occurs during emerging adulthood. In the current difficult economic climate, experimentation, though it may be necessary, is becoming increasingly difficult to do.

The twenties are the period in which many emerging adults cobble together career identities, that sense of "I *am* a (doctor, lawyer, engineer, writer, etc.)." Making this choice is extremely important, but those who are trying to help guide their emerging adults still have a lot to learn about why some are able to begin their journeys while others seem to become stuck.

Two Orientations

The work of Shmuel Shulman, a prominent researcher in the field of emerging adulthood, focuses on the question of why many emerging adults are successful in performing age-related tasks such as establishing careers, while others stumble, succumbing to feelings of alienation and marginalization. Shulman and his colleagues suggest that emerging adults adopt two primary orientations toward the career process: "doing-oriented" and "reflective-oriented."[6] Shulman's team concluded that emerging adults' career stories unfold along these two major paths. Understanding the differences between these two approaches will shed light on the dilemma your emerging adult may be facing.

Emerging adults who are *doing-oriented* tend to pursue activities for their own sake and tend not to be introspective about their behavior. They are "excessively active" in the pursuit of tasks they associate with entering adulthood. They tend not to show sincere interest in others but rather see others as interfering with their goals. They also tend not to examine their "doing" behavior very much and are unlikely to ask themselves whether their outer behaviors are good matches with their inner inclinations. This combination of traits can lead to confusion and stress.

In contrast, those who are *reflective-oriented* are thoughtful about their behaviors and their future plans. They are better at understanding their own behavior as well as the behavior of others. They thoughtfully examine their activities and try to integrate their diverse experiences in personally meaningful ways. They try to weave a cohesive inner story. This group shows less strain and confusion.

Although reflection is critical to the process, dividing emerging adults into two groups like this does not, in my opinion, capture what I see as the multifaceted differences among them. Also, the sample interviewed by Shulman's team consisted only of seventy emerging Israeli adults, all of whom had completed compulsory military service and were in the process of pursuing their educations. Therefore, the results, I believe, cannot be generalized. This study does suggest that focusing on external standards, achievements and milestones rather than inner meaning is not a key to career momentum and happiness.

So how does this relate to the idea of floundering?

Floundering

The term *floundering* is often associated with D. E. Super, a well-known guru in the field of career development.[7] His research still has, I believe, relevance today. Dr. Super associated floundering with a lack of *apparent sequencing* in one's job approach. The floundering individual uses a trial-and-error style, approaching the career process in a haphazard way, as opposed to those who choose jobs that build on one another in a logical fashion. Flounderers drift from job to job, feeling overwhelmed and lacking vocational and psychological paths. They don't seem to be in a process of self-discovery. They are reactive rather than proactive.

Dr. Super distinguishes flounderers from individuals in *moratorium*.[8] Those in the latter group take their time to reflect on job-related experiences and frustrations. They may temporarily stop searching for a job, take "time out" or work at jobs that meet their present needs (often financial) until they are ready to engage with a job search in a more focused and meaningful way. Moratorium is a conscious, reflective and deliberate decision. Floundering, in contrast, may lead to a period of stagnation whereby the individual becomes stuck in a dead-end position.

The realities of today's job market are quite different from past decades and experimentation, as it is practiced today, was not considered a viable option in previous eras. So Dr. Super didn't factor in experimenters as a valid model at the time of his research. The current realities of the workplace, however, suggest that a nonlinear, trial-and-error style *can* be effective, although perhaps less efficient than a logical, orderly progression of jobs.

According to Paul Salomone, an expert in the field of career counseling, what seems more important than the sequence—the outer approach—is the inner process. There must be periods of assessment, analysis and synthesis as well as the "soul searching" work of defining one's values, interests and abilities.[9]

Salomone's words resonate with those of Shulman, in that both emphasize the value of reflection. What characterizes flounderers, in Salomone's view, is their inability to "take stock" of their lives and reconcile who they are with the demands of the marketplace. Flounderers do not use their "drifting" in a purposeful way, whereas experimenters do.

Reasons for floundering may include:

- Poor coping skills. These play out in an inability to define and negotiate problems. Learning to cope effectively may be a greater challenge today than ever before, given the number and complexity of choices young people face.

- A poor sense of self. Finding a vocational home requires self-direction and self-responsibility. These important qualities are lacking when one's sense of self is not well developed.

- Lack of job skills. Learning job skills leads to increased feelings of competence and confidence. Skills nourish our capacity to find vocational direction and gratifying work. Competence breeds confidence, which, in turn, breeds more competence. Conversely, limited opportunities for building skills can lead to self-doubt and unrealistic expectations.[10]

When an emerging adult is unable to find a vocational identity, he is likely to feel he is less than his friends who seem to be advancing in their careers. He drifts from job to job, unable to construct a meaningful narrative, a connecting fiber that pulls the various jobs together into a cohesive story. This leads to feelings of alienation, confusion, depression and anxiety.

How can you differentiate *stabilizing* behavior (moratorium or experimentation) from floundering behavior? There is no decisive test, but now that you are aware of this key difference in orientation, you can start to engage your emerging adult in this discussion. Talk about the subject in a non-critical way with your emerging adult:

- Ask whether your son or daughter notices any shape or pattern to the job choices he or she is making. What consistent threads emerge? What aspects of his or her jobs has the person liked doing and what has he or she disliked doing and should avoid?

- Encourage your emerging adult child to tell you more of the narrative or "career story." Is it a narrative that includes a sense of control and self-direction? Does your emerging adult seem to be making choices in a purposeful way? Or is his or her story more passive? Does it contain a sense of stagnation, frustration or resignation?

- Notice whether your emerging adult includes major obstacles in his or her career story that are preventing him or her from moving forward.

- Ask if your son or daughter is waiting for something to happen before moving forward. If so, what is he or she waiting for? Is it something external and out of your emerging adult's control, such as an upturn in the economy? Does this make sense? Are there any actions your emerging adult can start to take now?

- Notice your emerging adult's mood and attitude when she or he is discussing career choices. Is there a sense of hopefulness and optimism or despondency and indifference? Does your emerging adult *want* to talk about the subject or would she or he rather not?

- Offer to help identify skills that your emerging adult has developed in past and present jobs and school settings. If she or he is open to your input, discuss ways that these skills might be synthesized into a more satisfying job.

- Is your emerging adult engaged in the career identification process or does your emerging adult shut down?

Play May Hold Clues

Many emerging adults will not talk openly with their parents about this subject matter. In that case, observing them "at play" can be very instructive. I published a study with my colleague Ilana Lehmann that is helpful in understanding your emerging adult.[11] What your emerging adult does at play can provide an important window to understanding his or her abilities to be self-reflective, self-directed and self-responsible, all prerequisites for developing a career identity. Noticing how your emerging adult approaches leisure activities may provide clues to understanding his or her career strengths:

- Does your emerging adult actively pursue hobbies and interests for which she or he has a passion? Are the activities generic or do they seem uniquely suited to your emerging adult?

- How does your emerging adult engage others during the pursuit of recreational activities? Is your son or daughter sometimes the leader or organizer? What sorts of activities bring out these qualities? Can your emerging adult be a good team member or must he or she always be in charge?

- Does your emerging adult create opportunities to pursue his or her interests? In what ways does she or he do this?

- Are his or her interests generally passive (e.g., shopping, watching television, reading, going to the movies) or active (playing an instrument, playing sports, writing)?

- What, if any, specialized skills is your emerging adult developing in his or her recreational life? How might these suggest opportunities in the job market?

- Are any of your emerging adult's leisure interests purely self-directed or are they always led by others or by programs (e.g., computer games)?

- Does your emerging adult do anything creative? Do any genuine gifts or talents reveal themselves in his or her leisure pursuits?

- What technologies has your emerging adult mastered in his or her play and leisure activities?

- Is your emerging adult responsible for his or her own recreational life or does your emerging adult depend on others to provide structure? Does your emerging adult complain of boredom frequently?

- Is your emerging adult able to make decisive choices about what he or she likes and doesn't like?

- Have your emerging adult's interests evolved over time, becoming more focused, complex and age-appropriate? Did this occur naturally?

- Is your emerging adult motivated to get better at his or her "play" skills? Is he or she moving observably in that direction?

Two Contrasting Emerging Adults

Emerging adults today have been given the gift of an extended time frame for reaching key milestones (i.e., marriage, children, home ownership). This means they are in a potentially excellent position to make informed career decisions. In many cases, that is exactly what is happening. In other cases, paralysis reigns.

Let's look at two emerging adults: Connor, an articulate twenty-nine-year-old man, takes pride in his accomplishments, including the way he navigated his non-traditional career path; Brenda, a twenty-nine-year-old woman, shows no apparent career direction despite a promising adolescence.

Connor's Story

Connor grew up in comfort with loving parents. Small for his age and not much of an athlete, he scored points with his peers with his keen sense of humor. Connor didn't excel in school, but he was seen as bright and inquisitive.

Connor could fix anything and, as a teen, repaired cars as a hobby. He was self-taught and enjoyed the challenge of rebuilding hopeless "clunkers." He bought inexpensive cars, fixed them and sold them at a profit. Connor also taught himself how to play the guitar and achieved a modicum of success working as a substitute for established bands in the area.

As an emerging adult, Connor started studying at four different colleges, quitting each of them after a year. His interests seemed scattered, ranging from medicine to social work to the arts. His parents were concerned about him, wondering how he was going to earn enough money to afford the middle class lifestyle to which he was accustomed.

At twenty-six, Connor held a series of odd jobs such as seasonal work as a construction worker, all the while playing his guitar for gigs. Playing the guitar was a constant for Connor, providing him with a sense of accomplishment and joy. He also liked hanging out with his buddies in the music scene and occasionally dabbled with drugs and alcohol in that setting.

At age twenty-seven, he asked his parents for a four-hundred-dollar loan to execute a "business plan." Connor had been at the beach making a leather belt for himself when a passerby asked if he could purchase it. Connor had two dollars' worth of material invested in the belt and about five minutes of labor. He was delighted to make his first sale at a hefty profit, charging fifteen dollars for the belt.

Connor currently owns two leather stores and has plans to open two more. He loves his life. As a hobby he acquires the guitars of famous artists. He has given up playing in bands, due to the time constraints of his businesses. He is married and has no children. His future plans incorporate investing in real estate, including ownership of a mall.

Connor's story is instructive in that many of his behaviors during his twenties can be viewed as random, irresponsible and self-defeating. At twenty-six, he could not articulate a vision for himself. However, we can see that there were clues in Connor's play to suggest that Connor would develop career momentum, albeit in his own creative way.

Viewing Connor at play in his teens and twenties provides insight to understanding Connor as a professional man. Although he was not able to "stick" with college, he successfully completed many projects that involved goal-directed behavior of his own choosing. He showed good planning, responsibility and follow-through in his recreational activities. Many of his interests involved teaching himself the skills necessary to become financially viable, i.e., fixing cars and selling them at a profit, learning to play guitar professionally, making sellable leather belts.

Connor was able to enjoy and learn from his play experiences. In those contexts he was responsible to himself and to others. While pursuing his interests, many of which had a commercial angle to them, he became totally engaged in what he was doing. For example, as a guitarist, he never missed a gig and achieved local success. His guitar playing required countless hours of rigorous practice, which he embraced. He was also invested in making the bands that he played with as great as they could be.

Brenda's Story

No one would have guessed that Brenda, an ebullient, gifted teenager, would spend her twenties drifting aimlessly. After graduating from a prestigious Ivy League school, Brenda floated from one low-paying job to another. She currently lives four hours away from her family and enjoys the bustle of a vibrant city. She has many friends, although she has been unable to develop an intimate romantic relationship. She assumes a fatalistic stance in regard to her love life.

Brenda enjoys reading and writing poetry, a hobby she avidly pursued while an undergraduate English major.

She states she wants to make a difference in people's lives yet she rejects career-related suggestions, finding fault with each option offered by her parents, friends and professionals. She provides elaborate rationalizations why each recommendation won't work. She is unable to identify a career choice that sustains her curiosity and interest. For the past eight years, her pattern has been to move from one temporary job to another, with no job apparently serving as a launching pad to the next one.

Brenda has sought the help of a career counselor and a therapist, to no avail. Some of her temporary jobs have led to more permanent offers; however, she has rejected all of them. From time to time she struggles with anxiety, which she associates with her inability to establish a work identity. She worries that she is disappointing her parents and feels a sense of shame.

Brenda's family is successful vocationally. They are ambitious and enjoy competing against themselves and others. Her mother and father hold prestigious positions. Her two older brothers are launched professionally and each is satisfied in his career. Brenda feels she is falling short of her promise, but she can't seem to "get it together" and develop a career for herself.

What obstacles are getting in the way of Brenda being able to find a career in line with her abilities? What steps might be taken to provide her with a greater degree of meaning and gratification? With the brief history you have read, what are your thoughts? What would you do if Brenda were your daughter? How would you try to support her?

Brenda seems stuck in a pattern that limits her ability to explore and actualize a career identity. She is inundated with career possibilities but immobilized by fears that she will either be disappointed or disappointing to her family. This is an all-too-common version of "analysis paralysis" that is shared by many emerging adults. Her anxiety increases and she becomes paralyzed by information overload and fears of inadequacy. She then avoids the "soul searching" work of defining her values, needs, abilities and interests independent of her family. These feelings keep her in a stuck position. It is important to note that high levels of anxiety typically go hand-in-hand with avoidance behavior.

A Model for Looking at Career Indecision

A career indecision model proposed by Purdue University vocational experts Kevin R. Kelly and Wei-Chien Lee provides a lens for trying to understand Brenda.[12] It also helps us develop theories about why she might be stuck at this point in her life.

Before we look at the model, it is important to remember that it is based on work with undergraduate students who had not yet "really" embarked on a career quest. It is also important to remember that college students are a relatively homogenous and privileged group that does not represent the full range of racial and ethnic groups across the economic spectrum. Also, the results are based on self-reports. Participants may have overstated or minimized their career-related difficulties in an attempt to present themselves in a more appealing light. Still, I think it has value.

Career indecision, according to Kelly and Lee, might be due to one or more of these causes (which I have adapted for our purposes):[13]

- **Lack of self-understanding (identity confusion).** Using Brenda as an example, she may simply not know herself very well. She may lack understanding about her own strengths, traits and skills and how these relate to the career world. She may not have done sufficient reflective work to understand her own likes/dislikes and the types of pursuits that are likely to lead to personal success and satisfaction. She doesn't yet know "who she is."

- **Lack of career information.** Brenda may lack good information about the job market and the career options available to her. She has not engaged in sufficient exploration and is operating out of full or partial ignorance. Because of this, odds are that she is limiting her choices or misreading possible options.

- **Trait indecisiveness.** This refers to a general character trait in which Brenda may be *routinely* having trouble making decisions. Usually trait indecisiveness can be observed in many other areas of the person's life.

- **Choice anxiety.** This term refers to a difficulty in making choices due to an overload of options. To understand choice anxiety, think about the paralysis that sometimes occurs when trying to select a soft drink brand at a well-stocked supermarket or when trying to select a television program from among three hundred cable television offerings. That is what the career market can look like to emerging adults today, more specifically to Brenda. It is often easier to make a choice when the options are fewer and stand in starker contrast.

    Option overload can cause chronic indecision. Brenda is a perfectionist in her approach to her career, an approach that exacerbates her chronic indecision. A nonadaptive cycle ensues whereby Brenda spends many hours on the Internet researching career possibilities in the hopes of finding the "perfect" career. She becomes overwhelmed and despondent, then resumes her search on the Internet in the hope of finding clarity, a strategy that results in increasing information overload and anxiety. In a study my colleague Ilana Lehmann and I conducted, we found that the amount of time spent on the Internet is associated with perfectionism and career indecision among emerging adults.[14]

- **Disagreement with significant others.** Often emerging adults are strongly affected, either consciously or unconsciously, by the preferences of important people in their lives. Brenda may want the approval of her parents, siblings and peers. A gap between what she really wants for herself and what others want for her may be a source of indecision. Brenda may be reluctant to discuss this openly due to the very fear of disapproval that may be causing the indecision.

If there is a "career-indecisive" emerging adult in your life, it would be helpful to look at him or her in light of Kelly and Lee's models. Which of these factors seem to apply? By identifying the sources of indecision, it becomes much easier to offer support and intervention. We will talk more about this later.

It is important to remember that indecisive individuals may fit more than one, perhaps all, of these categories. Behavior is usually determined by many causes and simple categorization rarely works.

Brenda and the Model

Brenda's story is a good example of multiple causes. She seems to have perfectionistic strivings along with high expectations. She wants to make a significant difference in the world. At the same time, her lofty goals paralyze her. She becomes fearful that she will not succeed and that she will bring shame to herself and her family. It may be that by not making a decision, Brenda thinks she is keeping her options open.

Using the model just presented, Brenda's indecision seems to be a combination of identity confusion, choice anxiety and perhaps parental disagreement about the way Brenda is managing her career. It is important to remember that Brenda's parents continue to support her financially. This may contribute to her feeling that she is not "in charge" of her own life and therefore doesn't have authority to make a decision. It is also important to consider that Brenda's anxiety is not only limited to choice anxiety; she has more generalized fears about her future.

Targeted counseling would be helpful for Brenda. She needs a better understanding of her dysfunctional and repetitive patterns. It seems important to get a sense from Brenda about what was helpful and what was not helpful in terms of her previous counseling experiences. A realistic assessment of her strengths and weaknesses, her overall talents and the skill sets she can build on is vitally needed. Brenda seems intent on keeping her options open. However, she needs to understand that by not making a decision, she *is* making a decision that may well close off options. Her pattern of Internet use also needs to be examined in order to determine if and how it keeps Brenda in a stuck place. Daniel Feldman, a leading expert on career development issues, explains the problem in this way:

> As individuals pass into their early- and mid-twenties, the effort to keep future options open can impede career progress as much as facilitate it. Since every career decision can potentially close more doors than it opens new ones, young adults may become too reluctant to commit to any one course of action for fear that some future course of action may be more attractive. Thus, like in the stock market, it is important to young adults to understand as much about when to *exercise* their options as when to accumulate them.[15]

An effective counselor could help Brenda see that while closing off options does involve a degree of loss, there are gains including, perhaps, an increased sense of purpose. Effective therapy would focus on helping Brenda develop her own internal standards, which would assist in her working through the sense of shame she feels so acutely.

Family counseling might also be helpful in this case to deal with Brenda's longstanding dependency on her parents, including financial support. This support is likely contributing to her stuck position. Although Brenda says she enjoys the support of her family, that very support likely leaves her feeling unable to meet either their expectations or her own. Developing a stronger sense of self appears to be a primary goal for Brenda.

A lack of career information may be at play here too. Perhaps Brenda is not seeing all of her options. For example, one possible scenario might include channeling her interest in poetry by teaching the subject as a volunteer to a community of adults or children. Or, if her skills are strong enough, teaching a course at a community college. Brenda needs to engage in an honest appraisal of her skills, talents, values and goals while considering how these can interface with the marketplace. Career counseling might be of great benefit in this regard.

Choice Anxiety and Choice Selection

Before we revisit the five-part model, the idea of choice anxiety merits closer attention. While choice anxiety is not a new phenomenon, it certainly seems to be a signature issue for our era. From cable television to big box superstores to the Internet, never before have so many choices been offered to so many.[16] Universities and vocational schools offer an unprecedented number of career training options. Career websites feature a mind-numbing smorgasbord of job specializations. It is not surprising that career choice is becoming harder, not easier, for many emerging adults. Dan Ariely, a behavioral economist and author of *Predictably Irrational: The Hidden Forces that Shape Our Decisions,* provides important insights about choice selection. He asks, "What is it about options that are so difficult for us? Why do we feel compelled to keep as many doors open as possible, even at greater expense? Why can't we simply commit ourselves?"[17] Ariely and his colleague from Yale University, Jiwoong Shin, designed fascinating computer simulation games to answer these questions.

Using clever experimental designs, they demonstrated that under certain conditions of choice, people behave in ways that are not in their best interests. Participants (students at the Massachusetts Institute of Technology) were presented with three doors on a computer screen. Clicking on any of the doors opened that door. Once within each "room" the participant could collect various sums of money, one click at a time. Each room contained a different total sum of money. The player could switch rooms at any time, looking for a bigger money pool, but it cost a click to switch rooms. A set number of clicks was allotted per game. The goal of the game was to find the room with the biggest payoff and earn as much money as possible.

Ariely wanted to know, What do people do when their options begin to close down? Do they let the options go or do they try to keep them open, even to the point of sacrificing guaranteed payoffs? So Ariely added this twist to the game. After twelve clicks, any of the three doors, if left unvisited, disappeared. What did the players do? They skipped from one door to another in a way that was both stressful and uneconomical. Each switch of doors cost a click, for which no money was earned. In a frantic effort to keep doors from shutting, these participants made less money than the ones who stayed in *any one* of the three rooms throughout the experiment.

In another version of the game, participants were told that a door would disappear if not visited within twelve clicks. However, clicking on the space where the door had formerly been brought the door back without any penalties. Results were intriguing.

Even when participants knew that there would be no cost associated with making a vanished door reappear, they wasted clicks trying to prevent doors from disappearing. Ariely argues that people's desire to avoid the immediate pain of watching an option disappear can outweigh the gain they would get from just letting it close. As Ariely says in John Tierney's *New York Times* article "The Advantage of Closing a Few Doors": "Closing a door on an option is experienced as a loss, and people are willing to pay a price to avoid the emotion of loss." Tierney goes on to state, "In the experiment, the price was easy to measure in lost cash. In life, the costs are less obvious—wasted time, missed opportunities."[18]

Ariely points out that at times it is best to close doors and stop obsessively weighing options:

> Running helter-skelter to keep doors from closing is a fool's game…We have an irrational compulsion to keep doors open. It's just the way we're wired. But that doesn't mean we shouldn't try to close them.[19]

This experiment provides a graphic demonstration that people can sometimes keep options open for too long. For emphasis, Ariely offers a story inspired by the French philosopher Jean Buridan in which a hungry donkey stands in a barn with two identical haystacks trying to decide from which to eat. His indecision leads to his starvation.[20]

Though it is "human nature" to protect our options, sometimes understanding that there is a concrete cost for keeping them open too long can be enough to help an emerging adult make a more timely decision.

Solutions in the Model

Understanding is the gift that Kelly and Lee's model gives us. If we can better *understand* the reasons for emerging adults' career indecisions, then the steps for solving the problem become easier to figure out. Not easy, but *easier*. If your emerging adult seems to be suffering from chronic indecision, think about him or her in relation to the five-part model. Which of the five causes seem most relevant in thinking about your son or daughter? Do more than one of them apply? There may be seeds of solutions in each of these five problems:

- **Lack of self-understanding (identity confusion).** If your emerging adult seems to lack self-knowledge, that may be because she or he has been sheltered or overprotected. As a parent, you must force yourself to back off. Allow your emerging adult to make mistakes and grow from them. Encourage your son or daughter to get his or her own apartment, for example, or to carve out an adult life within your home. One of the best ways emerging adults get to know themselves is through making choices and living with the consequences.

  Perhaps your emerging adult would benefit from professional counseling. This can often provide a sense of purpose and self-understanding. Perhaps personality testing, administered by a career center, would help your emerging adult gain a better sense of his or her desires, traits and talents.

  New experience is also a powerful teacher about the self, especially if there is an element of risk involved. Anything that throws a person out of his or her comfort zone will increase self-knowledge dramatically. Perhaps a stint in the Peace Corps or the military, travel abroad or a summer spent hiking would help. These challenging environments facilitate the capacity to shift and learn new things about oneself. Self-understanding flows from being "tested."

- **Lack of career information.** If your emerging adult seems to be operating in an information vacuum (or overload, which comes down to the same thing), perhaps visiting a career counseling center will be helpful. Many cities and towns have centers that operate free of charge. As a general rule, encourage your emerging adult to gather career data from sources other than you. Your adult child may perceive information coming from you as thinly-disguised advice and may not receive it gratefully.

  Most high schools and colleges have job placement and/or career counseling offices that their graduates can use. Try to ascertain whether there is an inherent conflict of interest, as these career centers may be incentivized to propel their clients to pursue higher education degrees. It is a possibility but not certain.

  Look for career lectures and workshops in the hometown in which your son or daughter lives. Or, if your emerging adult is open to this, offer to spend one evening a week with him or her doing online career research. Make it a firm commitment.

- **Trait indecisiveness.** Is your emerging adult habitually prone to indecision? Have you noticed this tendency most of his or her life? If your emerging adult has a habit of indecisiveness, what makes you think your emerging adult will suddenly become decisive when it comes to a career? It is overly optimistic to expect someone who has trouble deciding about trivial matters to be able to make decisions about something as complex and important as a career.

One way to work with trait indecision is to look at what has worked for your child in the past. Presumably, your emerging adult has been able to make some good decisions. What was the catalyst or strategy for making a good decision in the past? Might a similar strategy be used now?

Sometimes parental interventions can help. I spoke to a father, Patrick Owens, whose twenty-four-year old daughter Kaitlin had been floundering since college. He and his wife Denise didn't think it was appropriate for them to be steering Kaitlin toward a career choice, so they tried a hands-off approach. Months of indecision turned into years, with no meaningful movement or experimentation on their daughter's part.

One day, while out walking, the parents came to an epiphany: "Kaitlin can't decide what color socks to buy; what makes us think she is ever going to make a career decision?" The parents went home and started doing research. Knowing their daughter had a talent for storytelling and fantasy art as well as a passion for computer gaming, they found a master's program in game design at a respected university. They presented their recommendation to their daughter. She seemed relieved to have the "decision" made for her and to have her parents' support in pursuing her true passion. She dove into the application process. She is now happily enrolled in the program, doing well and feeling optimistic about her future.

Is this a good strategy to use with most twenty-four-year-olds? No. But one works with the grain of one's emerging adults (more about working with the grain in the concluding chapter). Recognizing their daughter's chronic indecisiveness and inability to structure a path for herself, Patrick and Denise did what they felt was necessary to motivate Kaitlin to move forward in finding a career. In this case it seems to have worked.

- **Choice anxiety.** If your emerging adult has been stymied into indecision by an overload of options, you might try to help her see the costs associated with keeping options open indefinitely. Point out that taking action toward a particular career will not lock her irreversibly onto that path. She can always change her mind later if it isn't working. Help her to see that taking action is a tool for exploring options, rather than for closing them down. If she tries a certain vocation and hates it, that should not be seen as a mistake. Rather, she has gained valuable information that will steer her toward the right decision.

- **Disagreement with significant others.** One of the reasons your emerging adult may not be making a decision is that you or someone else close to him or her has very different ideas for his or her career. Unable to resolve this dispute, your emerging adult lapses into indecision.

Self-honesty on your part is required here. Are you, as a parent, trying to impose *your* career wishes on your emerging adult? Are you disapproving of his? You might be doing this in blatant or subtle ways. If so, you need to retract your opinions and do everything you can to show your emerging adult that you support him making his own decision. By owning his choice, he will feel increasingly confident about his choices and be able to accrue self-knowledge and good judgment in the process.

Is someone else in your emerging adult's life causing the disagreement? See if you can uncover that source of tension. Give your child strong support in choosing the career path he wants. In time, he will likely find the courage to make the choice.

Your emerging adult may be making a conscious decision to pursue a non-challenging career path for the present—perhaps to save money or to work on another aspect of his life, such as relationships or creative pursuits. Or he wants to step back and gain life perspective. By engaging in honest discussions with him (and with yourself and your support system), you may be able to discover whether your emerging adult is using his present experiences in a positive, forward-looking way or is floundering.

The career-related behaviors of emerging adults need to be viewed with a fresh perspective and parents must be careful not to rush to judgment or overprotect. Although some emerging adults seem to find a career identity effortlessly, many of them face a longer struggle, marked by false starts and periods of seeming indecision. By understanding what may be affecting their decision process, with your new knowledge you can help your son or daughter over the hurdles rather than getting locked in conflict. My experience and research has led me to the realization that emerging adults want to move forward as much as you want it to happen. Believe it and offer them your steady support rather than disapproval.

Chapter 4

FROM THE PROFESSIONAL
TO THE PERSONAL

Much like the career landscape they are trying to navigate, the social and romantic lives of emerging adults tend to be fluid, uncertain and lacking in clear rules and expectations. The current generation of emerging adults finds itself tasked with a job for which it did not sign up: to create a new set of social and romantic rules and expectations that work in today's world. Their parents tore down many existing structures, but some new structures have yet to take hold. These emerging adults grew up without a model for conducting relationships. The rules varied from household to household. If they didn't grow up in a fractured household, their best friends or next-door neighbors most likely did.

Where does that leave this generation of emerging adults? Just as many parents did not want to replicate the marriages that their parents had, this generation of emerging adults is committed to avoiding their parents' mistakes. We cannot call what they are doing a revolution, because, in order to stage a revolution, one must have something firm from which to push off. We haven't given today's emerging adults a stable model against which to rebel. They don't have a solid platform from which to spring. The strong bonds developed between this generation of parents and their emerging adults also don't lend themselves to rebellion. It stands to reason that it is going to take them longer to sort things out.

Many of the values parents have tried to teach their emerging adults *have* taken root; for example, equal sharing of responsibilities between partners, waiting for maturity before entering marriage and developing oneself as a complete person rather than seeking wholeness through a relationship. However, the old adage, "Be careful what you wish for; you just might get it" comes to mind. In a sense, emerging adults may have learned their lessons too well. They have taken the messages to heart in ways their parents did not necessarily intend. For example, some emerging adults I interviewed now place career ahead of relationships and marriage in terms of life importance and personal fulfillment. There has been a huge shift, especially for women, who have traditionally placed marriage and family far ahead of all other considerations.

Many parents taught their emerging adults not to seek wholeness through relationships and now these young men and women seem to be seeking it through careers. Currently, we do not know the consequences of these actions. Existing structures have been torn down, but models that work in terms of building long-lasting, satisfying relationships in this era are sorely lacking. Will divorce rates, for example, decrease due to the increase in social and romantic experimentation among emerging adults? The answer to this question will be as complicated as the current social and romantic contexts our emerging adults are navigating.

When it comes to the personal and romantic lives of emerging adults, impermanence and fluidity are the norm. Social codes of behavior have disappeared and there are no clear rules of engagement. Consider this: only a few decades ago, the great majority of women married by their early twenties, without cohabitating or having a premarital birth. By sharp contrast, less than 12 percent of women in the twenty-first century are following that path. This is a change far more sweeping than the revolution previous generations thought they were leading. Living together unmarried is now the most common social union for men and women under age twenty-four. Cohabitation has replaced marriage as the social norm.[1]

Most emerging adults I interviewed believe that moving in together before marriage is a way of averting the possibility of divorce. However, this belief is not supported by research: couples who elect to cohabitate are actually more likely to become divorced. This reality cannot be attributed exclusively to individual factors such as religion, socioeconomic status, politics or education. The facts suggest a more complicated and nuanced picture. The timing of cohabitation and the meaning it holds for emerging adults who elect to cohabitate is key to understanding the relationship between cohabitation and divorce.[2]

Couples who live together after becoming engaged are more committed and less inclined to divorce in comparison to those couples who elect to live together before marriage without the formality of engagement, a public declaration of one's commitment to another. It is a more deliberate act and appears to arm both members of the couple to defend against inertia in terms of staying together despite difficulties in the relationship. Couples who cohabitate before marriage are "sliding, not deciding," according to Drs. Scott M. Stanley, Galena Kline Rhoades and Howard J. Markman. It is thought that without the formality of a public declaration of commitment to each other, there is an increased possibility of sliding rather than actively deciding to marry, a dynamic that leaves the couple more vulnerable to divorce.[3] While this interpretation is intriguing, further research is needed to corroborate these findings and explore alternative possibilities.

It is important to realize that for today's emerging adults, experimentation has a different meaning than it had for their parents. It is not necessarily a mark of youthful irresponsibility, as parents may tend to view it, but perhaps quite the opposite. When their parents experimented romantically, it was often a way of reveling in the newfound freedoms of the sexual revolution. In contrast, when emerging adults experiment, it may be a necessary path to self-discovery. Without a guidebook to steer them, they are forced to learn by trial and error.

The economic uncertainty of recent times plus the mobility of modern society provide ample reasons why emerging adults are hesitant to rush into romantic commitments. But emerging adults still have relationship needs. How are they meeting those needs? Friendships seem to have taken center stage.

Friendship: The New Marriage?

In the past, most adults in their twenties sought fulfillment of their relationship needs primarily through romance and marriage. That has changed: In today's highly mobile environment, *friendships* bring the meaning, balance and support that many emerging adults seek. Friendships have become an extended "family of choice" for emerging adults. They provide many of the social and emotional needs that romantic relationships and marriage once did.

Colette, twenty-six years old and stressed due to grueling work hours, receives support from her group of friends. They help her cope with a high-stakes, treacherous work environment. Her friends provide her with a level of stimulation and entertainment that is a good fit, given her emotional and social needs at this point in her life. Unlike being in a romantic relationship, where she feels that she needs to be "on her game," Colette values the lack of pressure she experiences with her friends. Even when with a romantic partner, Colette and her friends date in groups. She finds it more fun and less socially awkward in comparison to one-on-one dates.[4]

Flexible Friendships

Friendships are typically flexible among emerging adults. Paul, an emerging adult unsure of his future, suggests that friends provide a good alternative to long-term romantic commitments. Reliance on friends provides a simpler way of navigating when one's life is still "in progress."[5] Fluidity, however, reigns, with friends weaving in and out of the circle depending on what is going on in their lives.

Friendships evolve over the years. Some stand the test of time; others don't. As emerging adults age, they value different qualities in their friends and many become more selective in their choices. Friendships are more likely to last if there is mutual commitment to a common purpose and values. Reciprocal support also cements the relationship. The possibility of a lasting friendship becomes more important as emerging adults mature. As emerging adults clarify their interests, values and goals, they seek deeper friendships with individuals who share their priorities. The process, however, entails experimentation that often, at least initially, includes more superficial or weaker ties.

One outcome hasn't changed for this generation: Once married, with or without children, many emerging adults have trouble maintaining friendships. The demands of a family and career interfere with their ability to stay connected. Regrets about lost opportunities arise. However, with the advent of technologies such as text messaging, e-mail and social networking sites, emerging adults can reengage with one another with relative ease.

Advances in technology allow friendship networks to persist and flourish, despite thousands of miles of separation. Friends can endure long periods without speaking face-to-face; they are able to keep up with each other's lives through social media. Emerging adults are able to continue relationships seemingly as though their friends have never physically left. A sense of loyalty to their emerging adult friendship circles, in spite of going long periods without direct communication, sustains these valued relationships. If they do physically reconnect due to shifting and ever-changing circumstances, friends are able to pick up where they left off years ago without awkwardness.

Many emerging adults, particularly males, travel together as members of a "tribe," guided by unspoken rules, roles and hierarchies. The tribe exudes a sense of "us" and "them." The members are like a family and are highly protective of one another. But they can be challenging too. As Ethan Watters, author of the essay titled "In My Tribe," points out, their behavior is, in a way, a new expression of traditional family values.[6] Being part of a tribe may actually help an emerging adult male mature, in that his fellow tribe members hold him accountable, in an adult manner, for his actions. Although tribal membership may delay marriage, it may also strengthen the institution of marriage, according to Watters:

What a fantastic twist—we "never marrieds" may end up revitalizing the very institution we've supposedly been undermining…Those of us who find it hard to leave our tribes will not choose marriage blithely, as if it is the inevitable next step in our lives, the way middle-class high school kids choose college. When we go to the altar, we will be sacrificing something precious. In that sacrifice, we may begin to learn to treat our marriages with the reverence they need to survive.[7]

For a minority of emerging adults I interviewed, friendships are sacrificed due to heavy work demands. The drive to get ahead and succeed in a highly competitive marketplace can make it hard to sustain friendships. Married emerging adults with children note that the work of supporting their nascent families places significant constraints on their ability to nurture their friendship networks despite advances in technology, a familiar scenario expressed by their parents as well.

Emerging adults tend to view friendships as an important source of sustenance and support, quite often the *most* important source. As emerging adults have increasingly deferred marriage and children, friends may function like a surrogate family, providing the support and love that was once reserved for significant others and married partners. Friends frequently find themselves living far from the towns and states they knew as children and adolescents. In light of the geographic instability this age cohort experiences, it is not surprising that friends create and embed themselves in social networks that facilitate a sense of belonging and connection.

It would be impossible to capture the social life of today's emerging adults without talking about technology. Computers, the Internet, smartphones and other communication technologies have radically transformed the way friendships are conducted in the twenty-first century. Not only are emerging adults communicating with one another to and from almost anywhere, but they can keep in touch with a vast number of friends easily and conveniently. There is no longer any reason, technologically speaking, to lose touch with anyone from one's past. Today's emerging adults easily maintain ongoing relationships with dozens or even hundreds of friends, from elementary school, high school, college, graduate school, former neighborhoods and past jobs. These friendships often lead to new networks of friends in an ever-expanding web.

Friendships that exist only in cyberspace are a unique development that may baffle some parents. My colleague Ilana Lehmann coined the term friendico (friends in cyberspace only) to capture the essence of these relationships. Emerging adults do not dichotomize and depict their friendships as "online" or "offline." Rather they engage in a seemingly effortless process of fusing these relationships. In a recent study I conducted with my colleagues Dr. Lehmann and Dr. Sara Tomek, we found that both types of emerging adult friendships—friendships with a face-to-face component and those that exist in cyberspace only—follow parallel processes.[8] At the same time, friendships that exist exclusively in cyberspace, at least initially, are not accorded the same level of commitment and support by emerging adults.[9] They are also more likely to end within the first year of the friendship; however, if they do persist over time, the differences between face-to-face friendships and friendships in cyberspace tend to dissipate over time.

Perhaps there is something about the sheer quantity of friendships that emerging adults juggle that gives friendship an accumulated *mass* as opposed to one-on-one romantic relationships, especially since the latter tend to fall away completely once they end. It is now possible to maintain an active social life with dozens, even hundreds, of online friends, past and present, without ever leaving home. The technology pervades our society and it is easy and fun to use. We are, in a sense, wired for friendship in today's world.

Romantic Attachments

When it comes to romantic relationships, casual is in; formal is out. Fluidity and flexibility are the major themes of the romantic lives of many emerging adults. Against the backdrop of the sexual revolution, new possibilities exist, such as hookups and friends with benefits. Experimentation with members of both the same and the opposite sex is not unusual.

Sexual arrangements of various types provide alternatives to traditional dating relationships. Frequently, the level of commitment required for launching a career collides with the time investment needed to nurture long-term relationships. For many emerging adults, the relationship is put on hold as career takes precedence. Yet sexual needs persist. So substitutes are sought, such as noncommittal hookups.

Fluid sexual and romantic relationships are the norm and there is little stigma attached to moving on and trying new relationships with different partners. The religious institutions which discouraged such behaviors are also less of an influence on this generation. Dating is much less formal and, with e-mail, cell phones and texting, plans can be changed at a moment's notice. As mentioned before, one-on-one dating has often been replaced by going out in groups.

Many emerging adults want to develop their personal identities before committing to marriage. Preferring to have a strong sense of who they are as individuals before entering into a monogamous relationship, they seek romantic partners who are also well developed and have healthy senses of self. The famous line from the movie *Jerry Maguire* (1996), "You complete me," is a sentiment for past generations. Emerging adults I spoke with believe that an investment in oneself increases the likelihood of a successful marriage or long-term commitment. This belief drives the social and emotional behavior of many emerging adults.

There is a tremendous amount of individuality within each generation. Generalities do not always apply. Although an increasing number of emerging adults are choosing to wait until their late twenties to commit to a relationship, a minority still marry before the age of twenty-five. In these instances, one or both members of the couple tend to be focused and launched in their career paths. The age of thirty (perhaps thirty-two to thirty-five may be more accurate), rather than twenty-five, seems to serve as the new "magical marker" for many emerging adults, particularly those who are more affluent and live in urban settings. Although maturation is a gradual process, emerging adults can identify a specific time when they realize that the dress rehearsal is over. They suddenly feel clear and confident enough to set a path for their love lives. Remember, however, the importance of differing contexts such as socioeconomic status in informing the behaviors of emerging adults.

Overall, emerging adults seem to embrace traditional goals regarding marriage and children. However, possibilities for alternative lifestyles that do not include marriage and children are no longer associated with stigmatization. What is new is some of the specifics. The majority of emerging adults expect that their spouses or partners will assume joint responsibilities for the household, both financial and otherwise. Also, the decision to commit to marriage is driven more by career status than in the past. If a change in jobs is in order, many emerging adults are unlikely to commit to a more permanent living arrangement or a romantic relationship that may root them to one geographical area and limit their options. For many, serious relationships are not embarked upon until they assess that their lives are "settled" and that they are more complete as people. Being financially stable is often viewed as a prerequisite for considering marriage or starting a family. So in tough economic times, it is not all that surprising that many emerging adults actively choose to delay romantic commitments. It is important to remember that cultural and regional considerations also play into these decisions.

Experimentation, rather than looking for the "right one," is the frequently unstated strategy. But again, we have to view emerging adults' experimentation through a fresh lens. It is not so much about "sowing wild oats" as it is about looking for an approach that works. Emerging adults view experimentation as a way to reduce risk. In that sense, it is an expression of maturity rather than immaturity.

In the view of many in this generation, committing to marriage without "sampling" a range of relationships leaves one vulnerable. Fear of divorce is ever-present. Experimentation allows emerging adults first to learn about the qualities in others that are a "good fit" with their own personalities and then to begin looking for mates who possess these qualities. It is hard to argue with the logic, especially when compared with the "logic" of past generations, which often led to marrying the first vaguely promising prospect that came along and then trying to make a marriage work for the next fifty years.

Experimentation is viewed by many emerging adults as absolutely essential to avoiding poor long-term relationship choices. Each relationship is a valuable experience that shapes and gradually matures them as individuals. Ending a relationship is not viewed as a personal failure as much as a chance for growth and opportunity to form new partnerships that are reflective of their developing adult selves.

As emerging adults speak of their relationships, skepticism and sometimes cynicism creeps in. Maintaining an imperfect match for the sake of stability does not appeal to many emerging adults. Sometimes emerging adults are skeptical about the idea of spending their entire lives with one person and view the institution of marriage as one where they must compromise their hard-won individuality to maintain a harmonious relationship. They have observed many unhappy marriages and divorces and want to avoid these scenarios at all costs.

The shift in emphasis toward career over relationship has produced intriguing side effects. While the subject of *passion* often comes up in discussions about jobs, many emerging adults speak of long-term romantic relationships with businesslike deliberation.

The goal is to enter into a contract that will be mutually satisfying and beneficial to both parties.[10] Clarity regarding roles and responsibilities is the key to negotiating a successful long-term relationship. Many emerging adults make the decision to become engaged only after a thorough negotiation process. Partners, both cautious at first, explore the day-to-day issues that may arise in the relationship and come to an agreement on how to best resolve their differences. According to emerging adults I spoke with who subscribed to this perspective, it is a respectful process that privileges rationality over emotionality. Rather than figuring out problems and solutions haphazardly as they happen, both partners try to *anticipate* the issues that might arise and plan for them ahead of time.

Passion doesn't drive many emerging adults, at least when it comes to choosing a life partner. Today's emerging adults want to land on firmer ground than their parents' divorce-riddled generation. Anticipation, deliberation and negotiation are crucial steps. Again, for many emerging adults, it's all about minimizing risk. Given what many saw of marriage when growing up, who can blame them?

Girls (and Guys) Just Wanna Have Fun

As most parents of emerging adults can attest, fun is very much on the radar screen for this generation of emerging adults. To some parents it can seem that the pursuit of fun has taken on an almost manic intensity. Why might that be? What are your thoughts about the urgency with which many emerging adults seem to be pursuing fun?

- Is it a natural response to the stress and uncertainty they are experiencing in the workplace?

- Is it a way to compensate for the seriousness with which they are approaching long-term relationships?

- Have emerging adults observed their parents having too little fun and working long hours, only to have their career expectations thwarted?

- Is living in the moment less frightening than living for the future?

- Is having fun a way to temporarily avoid thinking about the big and frightening questions that loom for this generation? These questions include: Do I have a financial future in an uncertain world? How will I pay off my student loans? Is the planet going to be safe and livable for me and my future children? Am I going to have health care, Social Security, affordable housing? Can my country deal with and decrease its massive national debt? How do we clean up the messes left by previous generations?

Many emerging adults speak of a profoundly uncertain future. They believe they have worked hard to get to where they are and anticipate years of working even harder for a future without any real security. On top of this, they envision making many commitments—to family, to job, to home—and anticipate that fun will be compromised. Fears of not being able to measure up are rampant. Add to this the fact that many parents have raised their emerging adults to focus heavily on themselves and their own needs. The intense quest for fun begins to make perfect sense.

As a parent, you might have legitimate concerns about the way emerging adults are seeking fun. Alcohol is often part of the equation and is often the drug of choice for today's emerging adults. According to psychologist Mark Fondacaro, drinking behavior is largely related to one's social network, not one's family.[11] Traditional thinking has usually focused on the family when it comes to drinking behavior, including hereditary factors and parental drinking. Although family history remains a strong consideration, we now know that the drinking behavior of emerging adults is determined to a great extent by their peers.

You may be wondering, *How do I begin to understand this attraction to drinking alcohol? Why is it so prevalent, even in the face of all the news about its adverse physical and mental health effects?* Michael Kimmel, author of *Guyland: The Perilous World Where Boys Become Men*, notes that drinking liquor in one's twenties is not only about getting drunk. It is about "all the freedom and none of the responsibility" and the "last hurrah before the real demands of adulthood begin."[12] I think this is also true for emerging adult women, although women with whom I have spoken also view the drinking scene as a venue for meeting men.

The social pressures are great, as is the need to anesthetize the pain of insecurity. The aim of drinking is often to reduce anxiety, particularly in social situations.

Drinking tends to be goal-oriented, according to psychologist Hara Estroff Marano, author of the book *A Nation of Wimps: The High Cost of Invasive Parenting*. She notes that the goal is to drink as much and as quickly as one can.[13] Binge drinking, which is defined as consuming more than five drinks in one sitting for men, four for women, is quite common among people in their twenties. Binge drinking carries many negative consequences. Among a range of problems associated with binge drinking, 28.6 percent of college students report feeling regret for something they did sexually while bingeing.[14] Binge drinking usually occurs with drinking buddies (for both males and females). The good news is that by their late twenties, most emerging adults no longer engage in binge drinking and drinking itself subsides significantly (with occasional bursts of excess). Many emerging adults state that by their late twenties the pursuit of careers and relationships takes precedence and that, physically, their bodies can no longer juggle the demands of work and partying.[15]

Although today's emerging adults may *appear* to be behaving irresponsibly, the perspective of some is that perhaps there is an underlying logic, even maturity, to their choices. How can this be true about something as reckless as drinking to excess? In the case of drinking, the argument might be: perhaps it makes sense to indulge one's appetites while one is still young and free of family and career responsibilities. By granting oneself "free rein," so to speak, perhaps the desire to overindulge in alcohol plays itself out, runs its course and diminishes naturally. Imagine a nine-year-old who is left alone in a house filled with cookies. At first he eats himself into a stupor. But soon he learns that eating a whole pound of cookies really isn't that much fun and begins to voluntarily regulate himself. In the same way, drinking to excess, along with all the embarrassment, regret and hangovers that come with it, really isn't that much fun in the end. According to this theory, when one learns this lesson for oneself, it becomes part of the maturation process; it sticks.

However, I believe drinking to excess is high-stakes behavior with accompanying compromised judgment (many accidents can and do occur in an inebriated state). Some emerging adults make poor decisions as a result of impaired judgment and the consequences can be serious, such as a car accident or an unwanted pregnancy. Others may end up with health issues.

Educational institutions are increasingly evaluating their part in enabling the drinking behavior of emerging adult students. Institutions serving emerging adults need to step up and not ignore what is occurring in their establishments. Attending college is associated with increasing problematic drinking behavior. The good news is that if your emerging adult can escape the results associated with problematic drinking behavior, including the availability of alcohol as well as the ritualization and normalization of drinking on college campuses, drinking behavior dissipates once the emerging adult leaves the college environment.[16]

Fortunately, there is more general awareness of the signs of alcohol dependency and there are better behavioral controls in place than in prior generations. Today's emerging adults are much less likely to drive a car after a night of partying than many in their parents' generation were. More planning, with an eye toward safety, usually takes place. Taxi cabs and designated drivers are often used.

It is important to understand and be aware of the behavior and mindset of your emerging adult. Alcohol is an integral part of emerging adult culture. As long as your son or daughter appears to be maintaining a sense of control and an awareness of the consequences and as long as drinking is not affecting his or her job, safety or relationships, it might be wise to keep a cautious "hands-off" policy and trust that your emerging adult's good judgment will prevail.

Fun-seeking in general, with or without alcohol, has a tendency to play itself out over time. As long as the behavior is not destructive or compulsive, you can probably "let the good times roll" for your son or daughter and be thankful that he or she is doing the steps in the right order—that is, getting the partying behavior out of the way *before* taking on the responsibilities of family and career.

Divorce

Whereas in the past divorce was viewed as certain to cause irreparable damage in marriages, a more positive or at least neutral view has been taking shape. Divorce is now viewed within the range of "normal" family transitions. It has been largely de-stigmatized. However, the impact of divorce is still real and for many it is not always benign.

Divorce is not a discrete event; it is a process. It often has positive aspects along with the negative. Typically, discord was present in a marriage long before the divorce. Under certain conditions, divorce can be a transformative experience that results in growth for all members of the family. Divorce can represent relief from years of crushing tensions and conflict and an opportunity to build more satisfying relationships.[17] For others, divorce can be a traumatic event that leaves permanent scars.

The security that emerging adults feel around their romantic attachments has been found by some researchers to be related to the emerging adults' own experiences with parental divorce.[18] For example, for some emerging adults from divorced homes, divorce may signal that relationships are not necessarily secure and that they can go awry. If the one relationship they trusted above all others—their parents'—has failed, then anything is possible. As a result, emerging adults may become disillusioned and wary when pursuing romantic partners.[19]

From a body of literature that is inconsistent regarding the impact of divorce on emerging adults, we can conclude that there is a tremendous range in the responses of emerging adults to divorce.[20] There are no set principles we can apply. The personalities and skills that individual family members bring to the divorce process have a large effect on the outcome, as do the home environments before and after the divorce. But the possibility remains that divorce may influence romantic relationships and child-rearing in ways that haven't been entirely captured by research findings. The degree of conflict is an important consideration. All people thrive in environments that are relatively harmonious. It is not surprising, then, that children fare better in harmonious single-parent households when compared with two-parent households ridden with conflict.

The story of divorce is a story of loss. How emerging adults *deal* with loss is a critical key as to whether divorce becomes a positive or negative influence. Laura King and Courtney Raspin of the Department of Psychological Services at the University of Missouri, Columbia, capture the meaning of loss and its place in the narrative of divorce:

A history devoid of loss is only part of a history. A larger understanding of our place in the world requires a more expansive view that allows for legitimate loss, an awareness of what might have been, and the capacity to reinvest and risk loss once again.[21]

One idea that was shared among most of the emerging adults I interviewed was that it is wise to have a number of romantic experiences before making a major commitment. They tended to feel strongly about forging self-identities that were "complete" by themselves (as opposed to the "you complete me" notions of romantic songs and movies) before getting married. It is clear that fear of divorce influences their views about marriage to a fair extent.

Most emerging adults with whom I spoke felt it was desirable to experiment with a wide *range* of relationships before tying the knot. The reasons for this were twofold: to ensure finding a more perfect "fit" and to avoid potential financial loss due to marrying the wrong person (and subsequently getting divorced).

Yet, despite their cautions and concerns, some emerging adults are divorcing, though they are in the minority.[22] In part, their decisions to divorce are driven by their expectations for marriage, expectations that differ from those of their parents. Emotional fulfillment and the abilities to be authentic and to be understood by their partners seem to be the new criteria for romantic relationships. Financial support is less of an issue. When both parties are likely to be employed and somewhat financially independent, lack of *emotional* fulfillment is more likely to signify the end of a marriage, particularly if the couple is childless.

In the past, motivations for marriage have included sharing household expenses, creating children and having sex. This is no longer the case. Living together unmarried is now largely acceptable in most segments of society. Emerging adults who *do* wish to marry are now motivated by the desire to be transported to a "higher emotional plane. And when that doesn't happen, they leave—facing little stigma and with few regrets."[23]

In a world where many emerging adults are feeling fragmented, looking to a partner to fulfill all of one's needs places the marriage at risk. Disappointment is likely to set in. Most emerging adults do not enter marriage with the idea that it will solve all their concerns and personal issues. They do not take the view that if it does not work out, they will leave. But given the high expectations described, combined with the quest for a perfect life, doubts can set in, leaving the marriage vulnerable.

We have heard the concerns of emerging adults trying to negotiate the changing terrain in terms of their personal lives. Advances in technology have had a major influence on how they navigate their work and personal lives. The next chapter will take a closer look at technology in the lives of emerging adults.

Chapter 5

TECHNOLOGY IN THE LIVES
OF EMERGING ADULTS

Innovation in technology is empowering. Solutions to complex problems can be Googled in a few keystrokes. Seemingly limitless information about seemingly limitless topics can be found within seconds. This gives users feelings of potency and mastery unmatched in human history. There are virtually no time boundaries in cyberspace. I have heard the Internet comically referred to as the Mystical Book of All Knowledge. It *is* almost "mystical" in its breadth, depth and instantaneousness. Granted, it is not a foolproof system; much of the advice has not been subjected to the scrutiny of fact-checkers. However, there is an ever-growing "self-policing" community ready to correct inaccuracies. Wikipedia, one of the largest assemblages of knowledge ever collected in one place, is entirely self-policing, with all articles written by unpaid users and all corrections offered by the same community.

Receiving help from perfect strangers—on topics ranging from the absurdly technological to the highly intimate—no longer seems weird. Michelle Slatalla, a writer for the *New York Times*, notes:

…I don't know anybody who doesn't shop online. Or who doesn't turn to the Internet for advice. It is a comfort simply to know that somewhere out there in the vastness of what we once so quaintly called cyberspace are other people who have confronted the very same questions and willingly share their know-how with strangers.[1]

Alexis Gordon, a twenty-six-year-old emerging adult, wants to end a romantic relationship. She weighs her options as to how to break the news. She concludes that sending a text message or e-mail is "too impersonal." However, she doesn't "want to talk about it."[2] Voicemail seems the ideal method to her. As she makes the phone call, Alexis goes directly to voicemail without the risk of a live conversation.

Presto, one relationship is over.

Now, with her plans for Friday evening suddenly open, Alexis logs onto Facebook to see if anyone on her "friends list" is planning a weekend get-together…

Technology has transformed our lives and there is no going back. New communication technologies seem to spring up like weeds after a rainstorm and with each new way of communicating, social rules are being rewritten and adapted—sometimes at breakneck speed. Not surprisingly, parents and emerging adults often experience these changes quite differently:

Parent: I was the last kid on my block to have a cell phone and I refuse to have a website. I had lunch with three people the other day; two of them had smartphones, the third one had *two*. Each person was engaged in the lunch conversation, but kept reading and writing on their smartphones. I thought about this a great deal. These people are the salt of the earth, polite men and women, yet I felt their behavior was rude. *Was* it rude or is there a new type of human communication style which has evolved right under my own eyes?

I guess it's the latter. I call it cyberthought. People who practice cyberthought believe it is far ruder not to get back to individuals who come up on their communication devices than it is to ignore the person who is seated two feet away from them.

The cyberthought language has its own syntax, grammar and definitions. It is sprouting into all cultures. Rather than cursing my lack of understanding of this new phenomenon, I now know I'd better learn it.[3]

Emerging: We love our CAT 5 wiring and HDTV and have to have it…We are by far the most tech- and media-savvy generation in history and we're proud of it.[4]

But the Bad News Is…

While tools such as e-mail, instant messaging, cell phones and chat rooms allow for greater access to others than ever, they also can barrage us with information overload and induce anxiety. As I was researching this chapter, I received a text message from my emerging adult daughter with scheduling questions about a vacation we were planning. Although I preferred not to be interrupted, I felt *compelled* to answer her (and I suspect she expected an immediate response). An unspoken rule of conduct has been established: I will respond to her text inquiries at a moment's notice, whenever possible, and she will reciprocate. How did this happen? I don't remember agreeing to these new rules!

Our ability to easily communicate with one another in a variety of ways, 24/7, offers great convenience and has many upsides. One parent with whom I recently spoke says that his communication with his daughter has greatly improved and deepened *since she left home* for college, thanks to cell phones, text messaging and e-mail. She calls him between classes to say hello, e-mails him spontaneous photos from her cell phone and text-messages him when something funny or interesting happens in class.

But this accessibility can have an enormous price tag. With nearly everyone having cell phones, e-mail accounts and Internet access, there is practically no designated private time anymore. The new expectation is that we are reachable during all waking hours. Emerging adults are always "on." That's a key change for this new generation. Socially, there's no down time. And this constant accessibility expands to the workplace. More and more, employers have come to expect that they can reach employees any time of the day and evening, weekends included. "Cyber" communications take social precedence over live ones much of the time.

It's important to realize that often when your emerging adult appears to be acting "rude," she is simply following a new social protocol that you may not fully understand and that she did not create. She is probably trying *not* to be rude to someone else.

Let's focus next on understanding how recent innovations in technology enhance, detract and generally impact emerging adults and their relationships. We will explore two main platforms emerging adults are currently embracing with fervor: social networking sites and virtual worlds. The psychology of Internet addiction will also be discussed, interspersed with real-life examples and analysis by Dr. Rick Houser, a counselor, educator and expert in the area.

Technology: Bringing Out
Our "Best" and Our "Worst"

According to Patricia Wallace in *The Psychology of the Internet:*

> [The Internet is]…like a huge collection of distinct neighborhoods where people with common interests can share information, work together, tell stories, joke around, debate politics, help each other out or play games. Geography may have little bearing on the way these neighborhoods form, but purpose does, and it has a strong influence on our behavior. People can belong to multiple neighborhoods and they can change their behavior as they click from one to the next, just as you would when you move from business meetings to a beach.[5]

Let's examine our "best" and "worst" behavior on the Internet: altruistic and aggressive behavior. What do we know about aggression on the Internet? Are we more or less likely to show anger on the Internet, and if so, under what conditions? Are we more or less altruistic when anonymity shields us from accountability? What are the conditions that allow for altruistic behavior to thrive online? Answering these questions gives us a window, if only a small one, on the day-to-day impact of cyberspace on our lives.

AGGRESSION

The Internet can easily unleash aggression in many individuals. When this happens, rationality cannot be counted on. When we get annoyed online, we can easily react in ways that are at odds with our better instincts. Our darker, more aggressive sides emerge in an atmosphere of anonymity. It is not unlike the transformation we sometimes see when people slip into the relative anonymity of an automobile. "Net rage," it turns out, may be even easier to trigger than "road rage."

What provokes our online annoyance? We are most likely to be provoked when we feel someone is attacking our competence, character or physical appearance. In response we may retaliate and raise the ante. The most common form of online aggression is writing angry or insulting text targeted at another user. This is sometimes known as "flaming" or starting a "flame war." Flaming tends to be triggered in reaction to a perceived insult or toward someone with whose opinion we strongly disagree. Flamers are seen as individuals who believe their point of view is superior to others' and are not shy about expressing it. Flame wars tend to escalate quickly, with each side trying to outdo the other in a way that closely mirrors the dynamics of road rage. The "attacks" are not necessarily personal, though they *are* marked by open hostility and lack of restraint. It's as if the participants temporarily lose control and allow their mutual behavior to escalate.

A more insidious and *personal* form of aggression comes in the form of "cyberbullying," "electronic bullying" or "online social cruelty." The intent of "cyberbullying" is to cause harm to a specific individual or group. Cyberbullies send anonymous or disguised e-mails and/or visual images with relative ease, minimal effort and little accountability. Cyberbullying is targeted and deliberate, not a spontaneous reaction. It can be likened to a premeditated crime as opposed to a crime of passion.

What are the short- and long-term impacts of "cyberbullying"? It is too early to know, but the phenomenon plays out across a wide range of age groups. Contentious neighbors have been known to engage in aggressive acts on the Internet. Among children and teens, cyberbullying can be especially harmful and have devastating results. A young person's social reputation can be destroyed almost instantly by the posting of private information that may be true or false. Photos can easily be doctored in Photoshop. Because the teen and emerging adult years are marked by extreme social sensitivity, bullies now have extremely powerful new tools in their hands. Numerous teen and emerging adult suicides, due to cyberbullying, have been reported in the press.

With the growth of communities that are not confined by physical space, acts of aggression seem likely to increase. We can move away from an aggressive neighbor, but it may not be as easy to move away from a cyberbully who can find us anywhere in the world! Bullying has had a long history. With the availability of new technologies, this practice continues to thrive in creative new ways.

What can offset our darker side? Unwritten rules of conduct can certainly help to temper hostile exchanges. As online communities develop tighter cohesiveness, they tend to develop more sophisticated "codes of conduct" as to what is tolerated within them. Those members wishing to remain in good standing with their communities cannot act out with bold aggression and boorishness, for if they do so, they risk being ostracized. While many websites have explicit rules about interpersonal conduct, it is the *subtle and unwritten* rules that often play a greater role in shaping behavior. THE USE OF ALL UPPER CASE LETTERS, for example, is viewed as "shouting" on most sites and invites negative social reactions, though you probably won't find this "rule" written anywhere in a website's official policies.

Understanding *how* the internet can stimulate our aggressive urges empowers us to exercise restraint.[6] The more we use this amazing new tool called cyber-mediated communication, the more we become aware of our own tendencies and "triggers," the better we become at self-policing. Many of us have learned the lesson of giving angry e-mails a "cooling off" period before hitting the "send" button. This allows us to craft a thoughtful response rather than issue a "flame," which can feel good in the moment but can also provoke hurt feelings and flame wars. The Internet appeared in our lives rather suddenly and has required a fast adjustment phase. Thankfully, there is evidence that this adjustment *is* taking place.

A controlling authority can also be an effective antidote to cyber aggression. Five states have passed legislation that specifically addresses bullying that relies on electronic means.[7] This number is likely to grow. The option of pursuing civil action against an individual who behaves aggressively online also exists.

ALTRUISM

Just as the Internet can trigger our aggressive urges, it can also stimulate our altruistic tendencies. Many of us are reaching out to others online via various forums, chat rooms and message boards. Both giving and receiving help may be easier online. Emerging adults, in attempting to be heard and understood, often find self-disclosure easier on the Internet. Anonymity can free them to reveal sensitive personal details, a choice they may not entertain when talking face-to-face. We can become less inhibited when communicating in cyberspace, take greater risks and say things we might be unable or unwilling to say in person. Strong attachments can and do occur in cyberspace, due in part to the personal sharing that often occurs there.

Internet support groups provide forums where generosity and compassion are encouraged to flourish. Emerging adults with concealable stigmas such as drug addictions or hidden sexual preferences can create therapeutic bonds with others who are struggling with similar issues. In the process, they can find self-acceptance, affirmation and validation. Over time, as a result of such positive cyber-interactions, some emerging adults may elect to end secrecy in their *non*-virtual lives. They may choose to "come out" or to discuss personal issues more honestly with loved ones.[8] Interestingly, many of us seem to be quite self-conscious about behaving compassionately in person. The Internet can offer us an avenue for this type of expression. In an anonymous, non-judgmental arena designed to encourage us to share our inner lives, our altruistic selves can emerge and thrive.

The sharing of free information is another altruistic phenomenon that is widespread in cyberspace. Look for help with virtually any topic and you will probably find it online, often free of charge. The fact that so many individuals work so hard, without pay, to provide advice and other valuable resources to complete strangers is a strong argument against Darwinian selfishness. In the anonymity of cyberspace, it seems, the selfless and generous side of human nature quietly flourishes. One could easily argue that acts of altruism greatly outnumber acts of aggression online. Your emerging adult may turn out to be less cynical about human nature, due in large part to the atmosphere of open generosity he or she encounters online on a daily basis.

Computer-mediated communication provides us with access to a much larger world, rich with resources and a wide array of possibilities to engage with others in new and creative ways. Although it is neither inherently "good" nor "bad," computer-mediated communication can be *used* as a positive or negative force. Online we display both our best and worst possible selves. Both altruistic and aggressive behaviors are more easily unleashed. Harnessing and utilizing the power of computer-mediated communication, and rewriting the rules of social behavior that go along with it, will be a major challenge for years to come.

What we may not fully realize is that because our emerging adults are more immersed, and more fluent, in new technologies than we are, *they* are the ones taking the lead in rewriting those rules. When it comes to communication in the twenty-first century, our kids are teaching *us*. The rules are being rewritten and *we* are not doing the rewriting. So while we may be tempted to lecture our emerging adults about what is appropriate behavior with cell phones and e-mails, our opinion, in a very real sense, is quickly becoming irrelevant. As the "owners" and native adopters of the new technologies, our emerging adults may, in fact, know more about what is "appropriate" than we do. Business, commerce and social norms are shifting quickly in their direction, not ours.

With that shift in mind, let's move forward to two popular platforms among emerging adults: social networking and gaming.

The Facebook Generation: Building Communities

How many friends do you have? Facebook, the most popular social networking site, gives new meaning to the word "friend." It is not unusual to count over 1,000 friends on Facebook, a site that allows you to have as many as 5,000. On customized pages, individuals display virtual presentations of themselves, including information about their relationships with one another. To a large extent, you are defined by who your friends are. Facebook has over one billion users and is growing. The majority of Facebook users do not belong to the community of college students for whom the site was originally designed.[9]

The idea of Facebook and other online social networking sites is to dissolve barriers among individuals. In becoming a "friend," you can instantly learn about the other person, his or her thoughts, feelings and musings, and view personal photographs and other media materials to enhance the experience. Friends "watch over" each other, with the degree and intensity of relationships varying based on need. Facebook is a community with built-in flexibility. It typically includes individuals a member sees every day as well as those they connect with exclusively through the site. You can develop and sustain relationships with much less effort than non-virtual friendships might require. On Facebook, the mosaic of your life is displayed and your various relationships are "worked" and kept alive. It is easy to see how this is very appealing to emerging adults striving to develop a self that feels whole and integrated. Facebook allows you to rewrite your self-concept and essentially broadcast it to the world.

The meaning of community has greatly expanded in this era. Maintaining a virtual community that interfaces seamlessly with one's non-virtual community has become integral to the lives of many emerging adults. There are no apparent boundary distinctions.

Alice Mathias, former *New York Times* columnist, and Stephanie Rosenbloom, *New York Times* staff writer, provide their own accounts for the popularity of Facebook. Facebook, they point out, enables us to indulge our gazes anonymously; its very existence depends on our ability to "dwell" on others without making our presence known. "Dwelling" online is a cowardly and utterly enjoyable alternative to "real" interaction, claims Mathias. We are entranced with this medium, because we are "bored, lustful, socially unfulfilled or generally avoiding real life."[10]

Facebook, for some, is a source of entertainment, an escape from day-to-day routines. It affords the viewer an opportunity to watch an evolving narrative unfold. "[We] can turn our lives into stage dramas and relationships into comedy routines," according to Mathias.[11] Similarly, Rosenbloom makes this observation:

I've always thought of Facebook as online community theater…we deliver our lines on the very public stage of friends' walls or photo albums. And because every time we join a network, post a link or make another friend it's immediately made visible to others via the News Feed, every Facebook act is a soliloquy to our anonymous audience.[12]

Compelling questions swirl around the phenomenon of Facebook and other social networking sites. Is it accurate to assume that the more time we spend communicating online, the less time we will spend talking face-to-face? As we stretch the definition of "friend" to encompass individuals we may never actually meet in person, will the strength of our "face-to-face world" friendships become diluted? Does the time spent on Facebook, an environment that invites casualness and familiarity, discourage us from interacting with others in a more intimate way? We don't yet know the answers to these questions. Mr. and Mrs. Bee, parents of Amy, a twenty-eight-year-old emerging adult, are searching for their own answers.

Amy is a struggling musician trying to build a career to support her modest lifestyle. She is working at a coffee shop to earn extra money. Her parents encourage her ambitions but harbor an unspoken anxiety about her future. Mr. and Mrs. Bee feel that Amy spends an inordinate amount of time on Facebook, as well as texting friends at all times of the day and night. According to Mr. and Mrs. Bee, Amy seems easily distracted in their presence, "not totally present." They experience Amy as rude and they are genuinely confused by her behavior. They wonder if it would be wise to talk with Amy about their concerns. Dr. Houser offers his thoughts:

There may be several explanations for Amy's behavior. Emerging adults are focused on discovering and deepening their relationships, particularly their intimate relationships. With time, they become increasingly interested in developing more permanent, deeper relationships. Amy's preoccupation with her contacts may be serving this need. Her apparent disconnection from her parents is in sync with the developmental milestone of establishing intimate relationships outside the family.

Technology provides greater access to other emerging adults. Whereas, in the past, emerging adults would need to meet in a mutually-agreed-upon location (e.g., a restaurant), currently there are no such impediments. The concerns raised by Mr. and Mrs. Bee would, in fact, be more worrisome if Amy chose to focus her social energies exclusively on *the family*. Her Internet activities are within the norm and do not warrant concern at this point.[13]

The popularity of Facebook and other social networking sites suggests that they are meeting the social and emotional needs of emerging adults and, in many cases, of their parents. Perhaps these sites provide a forum for us to feel like members of a larger community. Given the fragmentation we experience in many facets of our lives, this sense of connection may be important. We all need to belong to a community, to be recognized and to be affirmed.

No one is quite sure about the different set of skills needed for interacting with others. One thing parents of emerging adults may fully appreciate, though, is the way that Facebook and other social networking sites are often used to enhance "face-to-face" relationships. For the majority of users, these sites are not *substitutes* for a social life, but powerful *adjuncts* to a social life. It is common, for example, for emerging adults to announce face-to-face social gatherings by posting announcements to their "friends" groups. This method has largely replaced phone invitations. Another positive aspect of social networking sites is that most emerging adults do not lose touch with old friends, as our generation and past generations may have done. In cyberspace, they can and do stay in touch with anyone they choose, essentially for life. Thus, they maintain a far greater number of active relationships than their parents ever did. These relationships are "tended" on a regular basis.

In addition, online communities can *produce* face-to-face friendships. We often hear about the dangers of meeting Internet connections in person, but we don't hear about the far more common phenomenon of fostering friendships. Jake, one father I spoke to recently, told me about how his emerging adult daughter Penny made a close friend as a result of an online encounter. As a high school student, she had met a kindred spirit on a fan site devoted to a popular Broadway musical. When Penny went to see the show in New York, her cyber-friend (with both parents' supervision) met her in the city and they struck up an instant chemistry. The two remained friends and when the daughter was ready to start college in New York City, the former cyber-friend helped her get settled and even got her a job. That relationship has deepened and has spun off literally dozens of other mutual relationships.

My colleague Ilana Lehmann and I recently completed a study with 516 college- and non-college-educated emerging adults and their use of Twitter.[14] Developed in 2006, Twitter is a social networking tool known as microblogging. It enables users to express themselves and disseminate their views to a large and diverse community. Unlike Facebook, users are limited to one hundred and forty characters and their tweets can be read by followers and other users who are interested in the topic of conversation. Tweeting is one way emerging adults can build social capital and feel connected and validated.

We conducted the study to try to determine in part whether personality differences exist between those emerging adults who elect to tweet and those who do not (measured by the Big Five Personality Inventory, which was developed by Oliver P. John[15]). Our results suggest that there are no differences in personality between the two groups, with the exception of extraversion. A small but significant difference was found on the extraversion measure. Emerging adult Twitter users scored higher on extraversion. They also reported that they had a greater number of online and face-to-face friends, in comparison to non-users. The size of the social networks of emerging adult Twitter users, not surprisingly, was greater. We found that Twitter users were more likely to meet others face-to-face after connecting with them in cyberspace in comparison to non-users.

The concern that emerging adults have interpersonal skill deficits as a result of over-reliance on technology was not supported in our study. As we discuss later, friendships are very important during this developmental period of emerging adulthood. Emerging adults can use computer-mediated communication such as Twitter to build, enhance and deepen their social communities.

Now let's turn our focus to another popular platform that may be bewildering and confusing to you—online gaming and "virtual worlds."

An "Alternate Reality"?

Fantasy online role-playing games have caught on, particularly among emerging adult males. Social structures in such games, unlike those in the brick-and-mortar world, are well defined and allow for players to adopt distinctive new identities. In many games the player is also able to adopt various evolving characteristics, which affect the way he interacts with other characters and the in-game world. Success is defined by fairly traditional markers such as (virtual) wealth and social prestige. A player is deemed skillful if he is successful in killing opponents and conquering their valuables. Men in the emerging adult years are the core consumers.

Typically, massively multiplayer online role-playing games (MMORPGs) use simultaneous text-based and graphic communication. Gestures, actions and facial expressions can often say more than words. As with chat rooms and instant messaging systems, the user relates to others anonymously, using only a fictional character name or avatar. Eighty-five percent of MMORPG players are males. Eighty percent of these male players are under the age of thirty, while 50 percent of females are *over* the age of thirty.[16] Females tend to be middle-aged women who stay at home and use the computer as a way of "connecting" to a larger world. The average gamer spends twenty hours a week playing games online, an interesting contrast to the average Internet user who spends only four hours a week online.[17]

It is unclear whether or not fantasy games encourage the imagination. Some believe "it's the game designers who mostly flex their imaginations, not the players."[18] Yet some of the most imaginative moments can occur when players try to "break" the game, create their own events or exploit programming "bugs." In one incident, for example, a player discovered a programming glitch that allowed him to spread a deadly magic spell the same way one might spread a virus. An "epidemic" broke out on one server, which created a major challenge for the game company to solve. Executives were later approached by more than one university interested in using the company's game data to study how viruses spread in the non-virtual world.

Collaboration certainly seems to be a skill that is taught, or at least reinforced, by games. Groups of players can organize strategically and creatively to accomplish goals that would be difficult or impossible for an individual to achieve alone. The extent to which these collaborative skills translate to the real world is as yet unknown.

What we do know, however, is that fantasy games are extremely time-consuming. Hardcore "gamers," who are the heaviest users of online games as compared to casual gamers and non-users, tend to be those who are least fulfilled in their face-to-face relationships. To put things in perspective, Internet use is generally considered problematic when it exceeds twenty hours per week. It is not uncommon nowadays for therapists to see clients who report serious "addiction." As the use of online games increases, social anxiety may become more evident among users.

Using the term "non-virtual" rather than "real" when describing face-to-face relationships is actually preferable to many people under thirty. That's because online relationships are very "real" to the gamer and the social networker. As a parent of an emerging adult, it is helpful to make a mental shift and view Internet life as "real" for many emerging adults.

But when does virtual reality become *too* real? What separates a "robust hobby" from an obsession? There are no hard-and-fast answers but we will look at some good indicators in a moment. As is often the case among "addicted" individuals, however, it is family members, not the users themselves, who typically become concerned with "problematic" behavior. It is also typically family members who ask their emerging adult to seek professional help.

Ethan Gilsdorf, author of *Escape Artists: Travels through the Worlds of Role-Playing Freaks, Online Gaming Geeks, and Other Dwellers of Imaginary Realms,* asks an important question:

> "[I]s this obsession with fantasy heroics a kind of cowardice— a perpetual infantilizing, an inability to take real-life risks that actually [matter]?...I fear a massive cultural failure to fight real battles in actual, not virtual life."[19]

Do "virtual world" games leave emerging adult players more dissatisfied with "reality"? Is Gilsdorf right in his concern that the real issue might be "a massive cultural failure to fight real battles in actual, not virtual life"? Are gamers hiding behind avatars in their lonely bedrooms behind closed doors, or is this just a cultural stereotype?

The amount of *time* spent on these games leaves substantially less opportunity to interact with the non-virtual world. Skills gained in virtual games may or may not generalize to non-virtual interactions. Let's explore these questions by entering the world of Josh, a twenty-two-year-old emerging adult gamer, and his parents, Mr. and Mrs. Denoya.

Josh has been a loner most of his life. Although intellectually gifted, he attended college classes sporadically and dropped out after freshman year due to poor grades. Josh spends over twenty hours a week playing a virtual reality game, staying up until all hours of the night. He is currently living at home and seeking employment. He has worked in various jobs, moving restlessly from one to another, either quitting on his own or being fired. When queried about his lifestyle, he responds, "I am trying to find out what I want to do with my life." His parents are concerned and do not trust that he is telling them the truth about himself and the way he spends his time. They are very worried about his on-line gaming. Josh rebuffs Mr. and Mrs. Denoya's requests to be a member of the family, refusing to join them for dinner.

Is Josh addicted? How do we begin to think about addiction on the Internet?

A Journey to the Dark Side: Internet Addiction

Internet use/abuse has captured the concern of parents and professionals alike. It is important to remember, though, that Internet abuse has not yet been formally identified as a disorder by the American Psychiatric Association. While Internet addiction does not appear as a clinical disorder in the DSM-IV, the text of psychiatric diagnoses, there is growing support for acknowledging it as a legitimate concern. The new version of the DSM will list "Internet-use disorder" as a condition which merits further study. The rate of Internet abusers is estimated to be between 6 and 15 percent in the United States and it is anticipated that this rate will increase as the technology improves. Within college populations, the incidence of abuse has been estimated to be as high as 18 percent.[20]

Those who are most inclined to be psychologically dependent on the Internet are likely to show these behaviors:

- "They find it increasingly difficult to meet their major obligations at work, school or home.

- They use [the Internet] longer, with less enjoyment. They are restless, irritable, and anxious when not using.

- They do not succeed in cutting down, controlling or stopping use [on their own].

- They experience physical, psychological and social problems due to their use, yet they persist in their behavior."[21]

Dr. Kimberly Young of Saint Bonaventure University has developed a questionnaire to help people assess what she terms "problematic Internet use" (PIU). Dr. Young asks these questions:

- Do you feel preoccupied with the Internet (think about previous online activity or anticipate next online session)?

- Do you feel the need to use the Internet for increasing amounts of time in order to achieve satisfaction?

- Have you repeatedly made unsuccessful efforts to control, cut back or stop Internet use?

- Do you feel restless, moody, depressed or irritable when attempting to cut down or stop Internet use?

- Do you stay online longer than originally intended?

- Have you jeopardized or risked the loss of a significant relationship, job, educational or career opportunity because of the Internet?

- Have you lied to family members, therapists or others to conceal your extent of involvement with the Internet?

- Do you use the Internet as a way of escaping from problems or relieving a dysphoric mood (e.g., feelings of helplessness, guilt, anxiety, depression)?[22]

Answering yes to five of the eight questions suggests a problem with addiction, according to Dr. Young. Let's return to Josh's story and try to determine whether or not he is addicted to his game. Dr. Houser offers these insights:

Josh's experience with a strong connection to a virtual world is not inconsistent with what we know about loners and the way they relate to others in a virtual world. Josh can assume a new role and in that medium feel safe in his online identity. Participation in a virtual world allows him to close the gap between his real and ideal self. In the virtual reality environment, Josh can begin to be the person he would like to be. He can develop close relationships or feelings of connection to others, and establish with them a sense of closeness or distance that feels comfortable to him.

Such close connections may not occur as quickly in "real" life interactions, because of the perception of threat. Josh most likely does not feel as safe in his non-virtual world. Many times those participating in the virtual world feel they can disclose more quickly and at a deeper level compared to their non-virtual interactions. However, Josh's retreat into a virtual world can have a negative impact too, as evidenced by findings of interpersonal problems and mental health problems among users.

He plays a virtual game that is focused on competing and destroying others in a community...The participant is focused on violent activities. Those individuals who have an inherent propensity toward violence are significantly influenced by playing violent video or virtual world games. Josh's parents may well have a reason to be concerned about his behavior. It is important to know whether Josh has shown aggressive tendencies in the past. If not, Josh is most likely engaging with the game to meet a basic need of connecting with others without too much risk or opportunities for rejection.[23]

Causes and Treatment

What allows us to become addicted to these games? Are there characteristics specific to the Internet that encourage addictive behavior? The answer is unequivocally yes. Internet use and abuse increases with easy access and high-speed capability. The faster the Internet connection, the more impressive the graphics and the more responsive the game, the more compelling the experience. ("Addictive" is a term frequently used in the gaming press to indicate a hot game.) The opportunity to experiment with a fictional persona is an additional enticement. As with other online players, Josh is not restricted by his physical appearance when playing. He can be noticed, liked and appreciated strictly on the basis of his skills. In that regard the game, unlike reality, is a true meritocracy.

Interaction in online games provides players with social rewards (on the kind of variable schedule that B. F. Skinner showed us to be powerfully reinforcing). In vanquishing a formidable foe, Josh probably receives immediate kudos from his fellow gamers. He may also experience an adrenaline rush in his quest to destroy the threatening force. If he succeeds and "levels up" to a higher character level, Josh also receives respect from his peer group. Seen through this lens, spending lots of time on the Internet can be rewarded quite handsomely. Emerging adults can become online celebrities, respected and appreciated for their talents. The classic "nerd" can become a legendary warrior. Players can develop "guilds" and other communities in which they feel accepted, validated and revered. The lure of creating a heroic persona and developing a potentially worldwide reputation (these games are played all over the globe) can certainly invite compulsive overuse of games.

How do we recognize addictive activity on the Internet? In addition to the "symptoms" mentioned above, the effects of problem Internet activity include: loss of sleep, strained relationships and decreased productivity at school or work. With respect to loss of sleep, a study done by a major New York university found that 43 percent of students who dropped out of college stayed up late to engage in activities on the Internet.[24]

When trying to get to the bottom of Internet addiction, we encounter a familiar chicken/egg dilemma. Does Josh, a socially anxious emerging adult, turn to gaming to ease his anxiety, which in turn reinforces his alienation from "real" society, or does increased gaming *cause* his social anxiety? As with most chicken and egg questions the answer is most likely "both of the above."

Jeffrey Parsons conducted an online survey with MMORPG gamers to try to gain a better understanding of who they are and why they spend their time gaming. His results reveal that gamers choose this activity because it meets their *need for companionship and empowerment*. In the game world they feel in control and capable. There's an enormous potential "upside" for dedicated players, without the social *risks* encountered in the non-virtual world. Gaming allows for anonymity and experimentation with roles that are different from those in the non-virtual world.[25]

The players most likely to become addicted are those who place high value on online relationships and whose search for social companionship is triggered by feelings of loneliness. Josh derives the greatest degree of social satisfaction from his online relationships. Gamers such as Josh often view themselves as more "real" in their online personas than in face-to-face relationships.

So what do you do if your son or daughter is addicted to the Internet? The first challenge is to determine whether or not this is actually the case, not an easy task. The majority of emerging adults spend more time on the Internet and the communication grid than their parents. Some of the reasons for this have been discussed. Most Boomer parents probably have concerns about their kids' Internet usage from time to time. Frequently, these concerns are probably unfounded. Most emerging adults, even those who spend a fair amount of time online, are not addicted. As with other addictions, we have to ask whether the criteria noted above are being met. Is the usage damaging other parts of his life? Does she use the Internet compulsively? Is he unable to quit on his own? Does her cyber life take clear precedence over her non-virtual life? Is he using the technology or is the technology using him?

If you determine there is a problem, then you face the same challenge you would face confronting any other addiction—that is, getting your emerging adult to recognize and admit that there is a problem.

If and when you get to that point, a holistic and humanistic treatment approach seems best, in my opinion. An appropriate intervention might be found along cognitive-behavioral lines. This form of therapy stresses mindfulness and present-moment awareness, an approach that can be very helpful for people caught up in an abstract world. Treatment might also include the use of an approach known as motivational interviewing, through which an emerging adult can develop more adaptive coping skills. The idea is to develop and strengthen skills in other areas of his life so that he no longer needs to compensate for the lack of satisfaction he is feeling in those other domains. Part of the focus would include correcting misconceptions and erroneous beliefs about gaming. A continuum of services is usually needed, ranging from information about gaming dependency to more tailored interventions.

Concluding Thoughts

Facebook, smartphones, text messaging, all these technologies bring a sense of immediacy and fluidity to our relationships. They also have the capacity to increase our anxiety and barrage us with information, leaving us with too little space to think and reflect. Today's emerging adults are always "available" to the grid. A valid question to ask is: having grown up *immersed* in the new technologies, are emerging adults aware of the potential dangers? Are they like the proverbial fish that can't see the water in which they are swimming? Parents may not be as *adept* at the new technology as their emerging adults, but at least they have seen both sides of the fence. They remember a time when telephones were stationary objects and people communicated by mail and by knocking on doors. Our emerging adults have never known what it's like to live in a world that isn't fully wired.

Technology is changing the way we communicate in a fundamental way. Any feeling or thought can be immediately shared, without being processed first. Does this create a garbage in/garbage out scenario? Are we "turning into 'pancake people'— spread wide and thin as we connect with that vast network of information accessed by the mere touch of a button"?[26] As we think about these questions, it is important to remember that individual emerging adults use technology to varying degrees. While some broadcast their life experiences the second they unfold, others are more deliberate and cautious.

Mark Bittman, author of a recent *New York Times* article titled "I Need a Virtual Break. No, Really," and a self-defined "techno-addict," declares that the only space he can create for *himself* is in his sleep. His laptop shares his bed, as I suspect is the case for many emerging adults. He checks his e-mail before going to sleep every night. He checks it again immediately after waking up. Where is the balance in such a life?

Mr. Bittman recognizes that he may well have an addiction to "the machine." In response, he has created a weekly ritual, the celebration of a "secular Sabbath" that gives him space to think and reflect at least one day a week. Although Mr. Bittman is riddled with the worry of missing out on something important, he concludes:

> ...I do believe that there has to be a way to regularly impose some thoughtfulness...Once I moved beyond the fear of being unavailable, what it might cost me, I experienced what, if I wasn't such a skeptic, I would call a lightness of being. I felt connected to myself rather than my computer. I had time to think, and distance from formal demands."[27]

We are all adapting to the rapid changes that technology is forcing upon our lives. There is no question that we have become more empowered. However, technology has also made it more challenging to create a space of our own, a time for reflection and renewal. We need this kind of balance in our lives.

We are only in the beginning stages of grappling with the changes brought on by the information age. How many hours a day should we make ourselves available for communicating? How can we honor our cyber-contacts without being rude to the people we are with? When does our technological communication with our kids become a vehicle for problem-solving versus problem-dwelling? Rules of conduct are being constantly rewritten. We need to develop new rules that are explicit and reasonable and that clarify the expectations we have of one another.

Regardless of the technologies that emerge in the years to come, there will always be a need to create inner and outer social circles in our lives and to identify those we can reach out to when we are in emotional pain. Facebook, cell phones, texting, instant messaging, etc. have enabled us to "be" with others in new ways. Friends no longer have to participate in each other's physical lives exclusively. We can have a presence in a new, hybrid way. Yet, however much time one spends connecting in a "pancake" way, I strongly believe there will always be a need to connect on a deeper level. Technology can help or hinder that experience, depending on how it is used. Says Joel Garreau in a *Washington Post* article:

> The reason we've always carved out a place for deep human contact is because we deeply need it. Some contours of the mind are so firm they lead us to selectively defy the imperative of growing efficiency. Ultimately, technological evolution has had to [and will] accommodate to human nature. It can deepen or engender shallowness [or depth] in relationships.[28]

Technology will leave us changed, no doubt. It offers us increased freedom, but it can also cripple us. On one hand, we can seamlessly navigate our new communication options, enriching ourselves and our relationships, including our relationships with our emerging adult children. On the other hand, we can become fractured, overwhelmed and ridden with anxiety. *Balance*, as in most things, seems to be the key, for both ourselves and our emerging adults. Again, the mere fact that your emerging adult son or daughter has a heavy "cyber" life is not in itself cause for concern. It comes with the territory of being an emerging adult in the twenty-first century. The time to become worried, as a parent, is when balance seems to tip—your emerging adult loses interest in non-virtual activities and relationships; technology intrudes on his life to the point where he is rarely "unplugged" or she begins to become secretive and defensive about her time online.

Rather than leap to judgment about the way our emerging adults use technology, we would be better served not to rush to judgment. Times *have* changed and simply insisting on applying the old rules is an exercise in futility. If we do this then our point of view will become irrelevant. Yet, at the same time, we don't want to sit by passively and watch Internet addiction, cyberbullying or any of the other dangers of the cyber age claim our emerging adults as victims. A watchful eye and an open mind seem to be the right combination. If *embracing* the new technologies— learning how to text, share online images, exchange e-mail via cell phone, etc.—can help us forge closer relationships with our emerging adults, then we'd be pretty foolish to resist change just because of fear or stubbornness.

Chapter 6

PARENTING AN EMERGING ADULT

Insightful counsel was offered by the parent of a 26-year-old emerging adult. He said that becoming an adult, by its very nature, is something you must achieve on your own and that no one else can do it for you. As is frequently the case with advice, however insightful, it is easier said than done. Parents all want to be loving and supportive and avoid nagging, complaining or disrespecting grown children's boundaries. However, many parents are afraid that the more accepting and nonjudgmental they become, the more comfortable their emerging adult children will become in their parents' homes. But a part of parents don't *want* them to be too comfortable. Parents want them to be a little *un*comfortable, so they will be motivated to move on.

The movie *Failure to Launch* (2006), starring Sarah Jessica Parker and Matthew McConaughey, comically captures the frustrations of modern-day parents of emerging adults. In desperation to get their adult son out of their house, the parents, played by Kathy Bates and Terry Bradshaw, hire a coach to help them sever their son's dependence. Ultimately, the son does launch, but not without bumps and bruises along the way.

Those bumps and bruises—can parents avoid them or at least minimize them?

The short answer is yes, they *can* avoid many of the rough spots and often some of the others. But there is a caveat. Parents must be willing to brave awkwardness and self-examination. They must be willing to adapt to new realities.

Is nurturing or pushing the best approach? Should parents strive to be like the north wind of the old fable, trying to blow the traveler's coat off by sheer force? Or should they play the role of the sun, warming the traveler with gentle rays until he himself decides to take off his coat? Many parents go back and forth. They are as confused as their emerging adults seem to be.

Leaving home has never been easy, for the "leaver" or the "leavee." But in an uncertain economic and social climate, it is harder than ever. The rules are in flux. Many parents wonder: When should I encourage my emerging adult to seize the reins of adulthood? When does "support" turn into enabling? Should I *expect* my emerging adult to live with me longer than I did with my parents? Does that expectation then *create* the reality? What can I do to help my emerging adult be ready to leave when the right time comes? Can I have an active role in this or do I have to take a passive one?

The solutions are difficult to find. Parents need to come up with their own answers. That's not necessarily a bad thing.

Let's look at some ways of thinking about parenting an emerging adult that will help you generate your own answers, suited to your unique situation, and hopefully give you some encouragement and reassurance too.

The Launching Pad

As we've been discussing, in the past children left home at a younger age and by more predictable routes. If they did stay in the home, the reason for doing so was usually made explicitly clear—perhaps to care for an aging parent or to help with a family business. The phenomenon of in-house parenting of emerging adults, with no firm exit strategy in mind, was not a widespread social reality in the past. It occurred only in isolated cases.

It seems appropriate to declare that a major new phase of family life has emerged. We will call it the Launching Pad period. The Launching Pad period often stretches on for years and most parents are unprepared for it. They don't know how to act. There is no historical precedent, so, in a sense, parents must make their own rules.

Parents' relationships with their emerging adults may suffer because of the confusion. But parents don't want that to happen either. They may be troubled by emerging adults' reluctance to launch, yet parents still want to have healthy, enjoyable relationships with them. Let's discuss how this can be possible.

Finding the Right Approach

For those who are feeling flustered as parents of emerging adult children, here is a reassuring finding: Most relationships between emerging adults and their parents *improve* over time. Tensions ease, communication improves and awkwardness lessens.[1] Hold on to this important finding, particularly in moments of despair. Have faith that your relationship with your emerging adult can and *will* get better. Research shows that, for the most part, emerging adults do grow to become independent, productive adults. They do launch!

In the last five chapters we looked at the new realities that emerging adults are facing in their work and personal lives. As we discussed, compared to the twenties of their parents, everything is more uncertain for them, less predictable. Due to the phenomenal speed of social and technological change and the economic downturn, there is less clear sense about where the world is heading. Norms and guidelines have nearly vanished.

That can be a good or a bad thing, depending upon how you look at it. Parents find themselves proceeding without models and that may feel a bit frightening. However, parents have an unprecedented opportunity for creativity, innovation and crafting their own unique family structures—structures that actually work.

In the past, social pressure was on parents and children alike to follow predictable patterns: finish high school/college, get a job or get married, move out. Today, no longer bound by social expectations, parents can do things their own way without fear of being judged or condemned. That can be a very freeing idea.

Parents can choose to form stronger and more satisfying bonds with their emerging adults than ever before. They can create unique households and relationships tailor-made for those involved.

Let's proceed with that optimistic goal in mind.

As we get into the topic of *how* to be parents in the pre-launch era, here are questions to think about and hopefully boost your confidence level:

- What other times in your past have you felt new to parenting or unsure about what to do in caring for your child? Perhaps when she or he was a baby and you were a new parent? Or perhaps when your child encountered life obstacles unfamiliar to you?

- How were you able to overcome your fears of "not knowing" and remind yourself of all you *did* know?

- What steps did you take to protect, empower or advocate for your child, even when you were unsure of the best ways to do this?

- Where did you get the information or support to take such steps?

- What does it say about you as a parent that you were motivated and able to tackle such difficult parenting challenges?

- As a parent, have you ever realized that it is better to trust your instincts than any of the advice available from books, friends and experts?

- Who might have noticed your past parenting successes and would not have been surprised by them? What would that person say to you now as you face your current parenting challenges?

When you think back on your history as a parent, you will probably realize that, to some extent, you have *always* had to make your rules and judgments. From the time you first brought your infant home from the hospital, set her in her new crib and said to yourself, "Okay, *now* what do I do?" to the day you unexpectedly had to teach her about sexuality or personal safety, you have needed to define parenthood your own way. And you have probably been doing a pretty good job of it. You have undoubtedly made some errors, but you have learned from them and you have tried to correct them.

You have a lot more wisdom than you probably give yourself credit for. That wisdom hasn't abandoned you now. It's stronger than ever, because it's been seasoned by experience. You can trust that wisdom and trust the parenting *process*, too. You will make some missteps with your emerging adult, but ultimately, as long as you are committed to the process, the process is self-correcting. Whatever is not working can be addressed. Be open to the idea that it is a process and that you and your emerging adult have the resources to figure it out together and self-correct.

With that in mind, let's take an honest look at your present parenting approach. Is it working for you? What do you like and dislike about the way you are negotiating your role as a parent? It might be helpful to make a list of pros and cons. What are the things you are doing well and the things you need to improve? Write them down. It's good to consider them side-by-side. No one else needs to see your list.

As you look at your cons you are probably feeling pangs of guilt and incompetence. Don't be too hard on yourself; whatever failings you have identified, millions of other parents are experiencing them too. You are not alone.

A Common Mistake: Helicopter Parenting

As we look for fresh approaches to parenting an emerging adult, let's look more closely at a current parenting trend. The term *helicopter parent* has been coined to describe it.

What is helicopter parenting? Many anxious parents, unsure of how to encourage independence, find themselves *hovering* over their emerging adults. They become over-involved and over-protective. They micromanage their children's day-to-day lives. Rather than let their emerging adults solve their own problems, they intervene at a moment's notice to "fix" problems.[2]

Helicopter parents seem intent on prolonging the Launching Pad phase, despite protestations to the contrary. They have become such a notable intrusion in emerging adult life that the *Wall Street Journal's* CareerJournal.com reported that the University of Vermont hires student "parent bouncers" during registration in order to "redirect" parents and prevent them from attending.[3] Other colleges have taken similar steps to prevent such intrusive parents from "helping."

Although parents of emerging adults are usually well-intentioned, many of them, especially some with greater financial resources, have become infantilizing, controlling and intrusive. They create family dynamics that are more appropriate for younger children and defeat the goal of independence. Helicopter parents perceive their children as less than fully competent, so they step in and "handle" issues, thereby guaranteeing that their children aren't afforded a chance to grow up.

This pattern of parenting is increasingly common and resonates with the anxious, uncertain times in which many find themselves. In their attempts to micromanage, helicopter parents tend to undermine their emerging adults' confidence and autonomy, setting in motion a cycle of dependency that can be debilitating. Emerging adults who are "hovered over" are often afraid to explore, experiment and risk failure. Instead they look to Mom and Dad for answers, thus continuing the vicious cycle.

Landing the Helicopter

All parents want their children to be engaged, connected and self-assured. Parents want their emerging adults to be able to navigate the complexity of the modern world and to have the resilience to work through setbacks. None *wants* to be over-involved, worried and intrusive. They would like to "land the helicopter."

However, their anxiety gets in the way. They worry about their emerging adults' ability to "get it right," so they hover over them in a desire to protect. They may even have trouble distinguishing between support and suffocation.

But why is it that parents fear seeing their emerging adults make mistakes? After all, they should know from their own experience that mistakes are the greatest teachers. Why can't parents allow their sons and daughters the gift of committing major screwups and solving their own problems?

There are many reasons for this. The economic downturn informs parenting behavior. The stakes are high and therefore there are real concerns that second and third chances may be in short supply. Parents also value their children's dependence on them. Many parents enjoy playing the role of indispensable problem-solver. It satisfies parental egos. It makes them feel important and needed.

However, if parents want their emerging adults to be independent, they need to question whether they are sending mixed messages to their children. One of the most powerful ways parents can move in that direction is to allow their emerging adults to make mistakes without rushing in to fix them. This requires a conscious act of stepping back and disengaging from the fixing process. It may feel painful and unnatural at first, but it is critically important. In the process of solving problems, emerging adults invariably learn about themselves and become more confident in their abilities. Parents need to understand themselves—their own vulnerabilities and strengths—and then proceed accordingly, empowered with the knowledge that in many cases they are likely to err on the side of overprotecting their emerging adult children.

Their Needs or Your Needs?

Parents of emerging adults must be clear about their investment in their sons and daughters. How much of your worrying and criticizing is about your own needs and how much of it is about your emerging adult's needs? Madeline Levine, in her insightful book *The Price of Privilege: How Parental Pressure and Material Advantage Are Creating a Generation of Disconnected and Unhappy Kids*, offers this penetrating observation:

> Well-meaning parents contribute to problems in self-development by pressuring their children, emphasizing external measures of success, being overly critical, and being alternately emotionally unavailable or intrusive. Becoming independent and forging an identity becomes particularly difficult for children under these circumstances...
>
> [The process is] not aided when kids have to battle against parents who are implanting other, often unrealistic "selves"—stellar student, outstanding athlete, perfect kid—into their [child's] already crowded psychological landscape.[4]

It is hard to parent an emerging adult without the parents feeling they have a major stake in the outcome. But being overly invested in their children is counterproductive in the long run. Parents have to learn to let go of their emerging adults and not to be attached to any particular outcomes. Their lives are *their lives*. The more parents detach from the results that they want to see, the more freely everyone can breathe—mothers and fathers and their emerging adults.

Every time parents hear themselves complain about their emerging adults' overdependence on them, it can be a good opportunity to do a reality check. Are the parents really doing everything they can to let go of their sons and daughters or are mothers and fathers encouraging dependence by intruding, hovering, "fixing" and holding them to parental standards rather than letting emerging adults develop their own?

Helicopter parenting is not the only way parents keep their emerging adults in developmental limbo. Parents may also use dictatorial, passive-aggressive, indifferent and submissive approaches that similarly fail to strike a balance between encouraging independence and enabling dependence. But let's shift our focus to what *does* work.

Let's discuss developing a parenting framework that works for you. It is enhanced by the experiences of real parents of emerging adults and incorporates the wisdom they have gained along the way.

Finding a Framework

One of the primary tasks of parenthood is to separate or differentiate yourself from your children. But how do parents begin to differentiate when their children are still living in the home and when parents are acting overly involved, intrusive or meddling?

Let's look at things from a developmental point of view. William Aquilino, an expert and researcher in the field of parenting, speaks of the parent-child relationship as *evolving* over time. It is not static.[5] Being a parent remains a central part of your identity, no matter how old your children grow, but different skills are called upon at different times, depending on the developmental challenges your child is encountering.

Your child starts as a helpless being, totally dependent on you. Then slowly she or he transforms into an adult who is capable of having a relationship based on reciprocity, respect and care. Parents have to change in order to support this metamorphosis. Your job is to read the new cues and to adapt to them. *This must always remain an active, conscious process.* What worked yesterday may no longer work today. Most of the problems that parents create for themselves are due to getting stuck using past models that no longer work. Parents slip into familiar patterns and don't challenge themselves to change them.

The most important thing parents can do is remain open-minded, alert for new cues:

> ...old patterns of interaction may change when families enter a new life stage...The past influences, but does not determine, the course of future intergenerational relationships.[6]

Familiar patterns will continue to be part of your relationship with your emerging adult. Parents can't reinvent themselves or their relationships overnight. But they can and should look for opportunities to create new patterns of relating that more closely reflect new mutual goals. Taking concrete steps involves:

- Rescinding old rules regarding things like curfews, dating and room-cleaning;
- Expecting greater financial contributions to the household;
- Sharing household chores fairly and developing ways of encouraging this that don't involve nagging;
- Spending more time apart and doing fewer mutual activities;

- Encouraging greater privacy by making changes to the physical layout of the home and to certain family customs;
- Cutting back on parental services such as cooked meals, laundry and cleaning;
- Reducing shared resources such as food and toiletries;
- Encouraging your emerging adult to turn to friends and colleagues (not you) for advice and problem-solving.

Leaving home has always served as an important milestone, an opportunity for renegotiating the relationship between parent and son or daughter. It is trickier to renegotiate when your emerging adult is still living in the home, but still this renegotiation must occur. Parents must make changes to support the tender new shoots of maturity that appear. Your past relationship cannot dictate the present. You are given many opportunities to rewrite the story and you must seize them.

Emerging adults, over time, disengage from emotional dependence on their parents. This is natural. They become less interested in meeting parental expectations and better at regulating their own behavior, emotional needs and self-esteem. The more thoroughly they can do that, the better the outcome. Your job as a parent is to *allow* that change to take place and not to sabotage it by sticking to outworn patterns.

The final requirement is this: *Your emerging adult needs to differentiate himself/herself from you while maintaining loving contact with you.* Remaining emotionally available to your emerging adult while he or she is building a separate identity is no easy task. It can be quite a painful process, marked by bruised egos and hurt feelings. However, it is critical to do your best in this regard. The goal is to maintain a loving bond with your child while at the same time relinquishing parental control, "fixing," judging and directing.

How Are You Doing?

How do you view your relationship with your son or daughter? Is there enough room for him or her to differentiate? Remember that, unlike adolescents, most emerging adults are not looking for benign control. They don't want parents' help in structuring their day-to-day lives or in accomplishing tasks. What changes have you made in your relationship with your emerging adult that acknowledge this important shift? Can you think of ways you play your parental role differently than you did a few years ago? How is your current role different from the role you played as the parent of an adolescent? Are there further changes you might want to make? What are ways you might surrender control without surrendering support?

One of the hardest things to figure out as a parent is whether the environment you provide is nurturing and encouraging or whether it is hostile or indulgent. Does it promote the development of a healthy, adult sense of self? Author Madeline Levine offers possibilities for consideration. As you examine your own situation, are you fostering an environment in which your emerging adult is able to:

- Feel effective in the world?
- Have a sense of being in control of his or her life?
- Form deep and enduring relationships with others?
- Develop his or her own hobbies and interests?
- Value and accept him or herself?
- Learn how to take care of him or herself?[7]

Sometimes metaphors can help parents visualize the relationship they are aiming for with their emerging adults. In my work with parents and emerging adults, two metaphors come to mind: riding a bicycle and watering house plants. As you read the next sections, do either of these metaphors resonate with you?

Riding a Bicycle

In teaching a child how to ride a bicycle there is a terrifying moment. You have to let go and trust that the child will be okay. At that moment of letting go, you may be panicking. You may imagine your child being rushed to the emergency room. Yet you somehow get past your fears by trusting and hoping that your child will be okay. If she or he falls down, your child will get up again. Maybe there will be bruises, but in the process your child will learn to ride the bicycle.

Riding a bike is something you cannot do for your child. Children must master the task on their own. They do this best by knowing they have a cheering squad behind them, knowing that a parent will pick them up and reassure them if they fall.

And they *will* fall. Some of the falls will be painful. But parents need to believe that children will get up and ride their bikes more skillfully the next time. Parents cannot protect children from the pains of the mastery process, a process that involves experimentation, testing limits and occasional failure. They must trust that children will pick themselves up and learn from those experiences.

Believing in emerging adult children—that they will be okay, that they will heal, that they will skillfully "ride their bicycles"— helps parents work through their own anxieties and let go. At some point, blind faith comes into play. There is no other way. But the process is self-correcting. Emerging adults will fail, they will learn from the failures and mastery will emerge. A parent's job is to be there emotionally once a child "falls off the bike," *not* to catch the child or to cushion the fall. There are exceptions. If you anticipate that the fall will be life-threatening, catching your child or cushioning the fall is warranted. Your judgment as well as previous experience with your emerging adult will guide you.

Watering Plants

Here is another way of thinking about the care parents provide for their emerging adults:

In my private practice, I counseled an emerging adult client, Deborah, who entered therapy because she was having trouble launching a career and felt quite anxious. Swamped by student loans and with limited financial resources, Deborah had moved in with her parents. The relationship between mother, father and daughter was a loving one, but Deborah felt suffocated. There was a good deal of what therapists call "enmeshment," the blurring of healthy boundaries.

One day Deborah's mother commented on the plants in my office. "They look so lush and healthy. What's your secret?" I responded, with honesty and a tinge of guilt, that I wasn't quite sure, but I thought it might have something to do with *benign neglect*. I told Deborah's mother that I sometimes forgot to water and mist the plants or to give them proper nutrients. I had learned through trial and error what each plant needed in order to thrive, but sometimes I was forgetful or distracted. The interesting thing was, the plants appeared forgiving, despite periods of mild negligence. I had learned to depend on that flexibility. But more important, I had learned to *believe* in their inherent resilience and to respond accordingly. The environment I provided was "good enough." It was not perfect, but perfect *enough*.

Deborah's mother was intrigued by my response. She reported that in her desire to have healthy houseplants she meticulously overwatered them and they regularly perished. We didn't speak about the plants again, but Deborah's mother changed her way of relating and stopped "overwatering." Deborah thrived under these new conditions. Benign neglect did its job.

Too Much Parenting?

Given the lack of adequate social and structural supports, parents of emerging adults are increasingly being asked to assume responsibilities they had not envisioned. Two such examples are: parents of emerging adults assuming responsibility for grandchildren, particularly in the case of an emerging adult struggling with the emotional and financial sequelae of a divorce; parents of emerging adults overextending themselves and assuming financial responsibilities for their emerging adult children. Let's take a closer look at these issues that parents of emerging adults are now facing.

According to a 2010 Pew Research Center study, the economic downturn has contributed to a growing phenomenon: grandparents raising their grandchildren.[8] Working women find themselves seeking their parents' assistance in raising their children. It is an immediate, viable fix to a problem, an alternative to expensive, dependable child care. Reliance on grandparents, usually maternal, can be understood in the context of a public policy on the part of the government to transition women, particularly single women, from positions of dependence to independence without the necessary accompanying structural supports.[9] Therefore, we have seen an increase in grandparents' primary caregiving responsibilities.

Grandparents who serve in the role of caregivers tend to be women. Sixty-seven percent are younger than sixty years of age; they also are likely to be in this role for an extended period of time. Fifty-four percent of grandparents who serve as primary caregivers have done so for more than three years. They are also likely to assist their children financially (50 percent) and help with errands, housework and home repairs (31 percent).[10] Research conducted by Gillian Douglas and Neil Ferguson of Cardiff Law School suggest that these arrangements may well be exploitative.

> ...even these grandparents may resent the extent to which they have come to be relied on by their children, and to rue the loss of their own active retirement...Moreover, given the matrilineal bias in grandparenting, and the gendered nature of grandparent involvement, what the call to mobilize grandparents would actually mean is likely to be the further feminization of caring and the further alienation of paternal grandparents...This is not a recipe for strengthening ties with the paternal grandparents in the post-divorce family.[11]

Grandparents are being beckoned to assume responsibilities for their grandchildren's emotional, social and physical needs. The dynamics of families vary, as do the solutions. The possibility of exploitation, however, needs to be considered. In some cases, this may be one manifestation of parents continuing to overextend themselves on behalf of their emerging adult children.

Another context in which parents of emerging adults are placing themselves in vulnerable positions in relationship to their own future financial and emotional well-being concerns the finances of their emerging adult children. Parents of emerging adults are the fastest growing group accruing college debt, with serious consequences for many.[12] The 2.2 million individuals over the age of sixty who accrue college debt on behalf of their emerging adult children has tripled since 2005, a staggering rate of growth. Due to a variety of reasons including job loss, parents of emerging adults might find themselves in the position of not being able to honor their loan payment commitments.

Why would parents place themselves at financial risk? After all, employment opportunities for those over sixty diminish in the marketplace. What are the emotional costs to emerging adult children, knowing that they are in part responsible for their parents being in this untenable position?

Many parents "overwater" in response to the anxiety-provoking world their children are navigating. They want to get it perfect for them. But it is hard, if not impossible, to perfectly "titrate" children's environments. And it is not helpful, even in the long run. Anxious parents end up teaching their children to be unduly cautious (or to rebel by throwing caution to the wind). Overwatering is a posture that paints the world as a dangerous place that cannot be mastered without the help of significant others. I suspect that this is not the message that parents want to send.

When thinking about what "good enough" parenting means, *under*-watering, at least some of the time, is the best way to go. Create conditions that allow your emerging adult to thrive, but don't obsess over the maintenance program. *Believe* in his or her ability to thrive under less than ideal conditions. Build on your emerging adult's inherent resilience.

Reason to Believe

Both of the metaphors I have suggested carry an underlying faith that emerging adults *will* figure things out and that they will do so on their own timelines and their own terms. They will create lives that are meaningful to them if parents let them. That means allowing them to feel their parents' faith in them. It means backing off and giving them space to make their own decisions, *whether or not* parents think their children are right.

Children are masters at reading their parents' anxieties. And so parents need to focus their energies on trying to get those anxieties under control. They should try to learn to sever their attachments to things going the way *they* want. Parents need to trust that their emerging adults will master the task of carving out their own identities in their own ways, building on their strengths and gifts. *There is no better approach.*

Here are anchors to help you tweak or revamp your way of thinking about this developmental period:

- On average, emerging adults take five to ten years longer to make the transition to living in their own homes compared to their baby boomer parents.[13] Although they use their parents' homes on a revolving basis, they do make the jump to living on their own: 55 percent of the eighteen- to twenty-four-year-olds, 85 percent of twenty-five- to twenty-nine-year-olds and 91 percent of thirty- to thirty-four-year-olds are not living with their parents *and* are no longer attending school.[14]

- Emerging adults do commit to relationships and aspire to traditional goals such as marriage, children and home ownership. For example, among eighteen- to twenty-four-year-olds, only one-fourth (24.6 percent) of emerging adults are married or cohabiting. In contrast, 60 percent of twenty-five- to twenty-nine-year-olds and 77 percent of thirty- to thirty-four-year-olds are married or cohabiting. These statistics are similar among developed nations such as Canada and Germany.[15]

- The majority of emerging adults report finding satisfying work by their late twenties. They report finding work that they want to do for the "long run."[16]

Taking the long view rather than a snapshot view of your emerging adult during this developmental period can be helpful. You probably should expect a period of "waiting," a Launching Pad period that will likely be longer than yours was. That means you may need to recalibrate your timelines for your emerging adult. At the same time, have faith that your son or daughter will move on and assume the roles and responsibilities of adulthood when the time is right, developmentally speaking. Hopefully this belief will help you find it easier to manage the difficult process of standing by, letting it be and letting go.

Chapter 7

STANDING BY, LETTING IT BE AND LETTING GO

Wise parents of emerging adults realize the importance of standing by, letting it be and letting go. However, this is hard for many. Parents are socialized to be action-oriented. Standing by and letting it be runs counter to everything they know. It suggests passivity, which is an anathema to the can-do mode of being. Many parents find it difficult to provide their emerging adults the space to be, to make choices that parents would not make and to stumble and fall along the way.

What drives parents to be "proactive" when it comes to emerging adults is the recognition that there are inadequate supports built into the systems that their sons and daughters are attempting to enter. Many raise their children to believe in The Dream and they are desperately trying to mesh the optimistic beliefs they were taught with the harsh realities emerging adults are facing. Traveling alone and "privatizing" their perceived failures and successes, they may likely have encountered few constants and much debt along the way. Given the lack of available structural supports, it is not surprising that over 50 percent of emerging adults connect with their parents on a daily basis.[1] Emerging adults value the connection and support that parents

can provide. Taking a phone call or responding to a text and offering words of encouragement and engagement is not coddling,
nor is it helicopter parenting.

Parents serve a vital role at this stage in their children's lives,
because modern society has failed, in my opinion. Parents need
to offer their emerging adult children a sense of comfort and
predictability to help offset feelings of hopelessness. Emerging
adults are being asked to go it alone, without adequate social
scaffolding. In the job market, they are expected to demonstrate a high level of self-motivation and identity capital—self-
understanding, self-discipline and planning. Those who lack
identity capital find themselves unprepared to deal with an economy that doesn't square with the view of unlimited possibilities
in which they were raised to believe.

Many parents are trying to assume exclusive responsibility
for "fixing" this problem. They are also going it alone. But it is
too mammoth a job and the term *helicopter parenting* must be
understood in that context. The solution requires community
and societal interventions. The rush to judgment of emerging
adults and their parents is premature. The issues presented in this
chapter suggest a far more nuanced and complex narrative.

Earlier, I commented on the importance of evaluating these
parent and emerging adult interactions in context. I invite you
once again to view the material we will be exploring together—
standing by, letting it be and letting go—in context. You know
your emerging adult and your family best.

Letting Go

Only in an accepting, secure environment that allows emerging
adults to be who they are (not who parents want them to be) do
individuals become free to explore and define themselves. Letting

go of one's children is a profoundly difficult thing to do. Parents have ample opportunities to master it. If they miss one opportunity, another will soon come along. Any opportunity they seize can be a new start. Suzuki Roshi, a Buddhist monk and teacher, wisely stated, "We don't need to learn how to let things go; we just need to learn to recognize when they've already gone."[2]

Karen Coburn and Madge Treeger, authors of *Letting Go: A Parents' Guide to Understanding the College Years*, urge parents to keep in mind:

> Young men and women ask for little more…than a steady and rooted home base to return to, just as they had many years ago when they hurried back from their adventures across the playground to find Mom and Dad sitting on the park bench where they left them. To provide this sanctuary and still stay out of the way is an artful balancing act.[3]

If parents can learn to let their emerging adults *be* while the emerging adults are still in their parents' homes, then letting them *go* becomes a relatively easy step. There is a hidden benefit to this *allowing* that parents may not realize: In giving space for children to be, parents also give *themselves* space to be and, in the process, become more self-accepting. When parents stop holding themselves accountable for everything that happens to their sons and daughters, their anxiety levels plunge and they can relax into the flow of life. Parents can start to enjoy parenthood more.

Finding Balance

It is very difficult to find balance between encouraging emerging adults to "lead their own lives" while also continuing to provide parental support. Given how difficult this process is, parents may vacillate between doing too much and not doing enough.

The nature of balancing is that it is an ongoing process. It is not something parents get right once and then walk away from. It is a zigging and zagging affair. Parents notice they're doing too much of this, so they try more of that. A freeze-frame at any single moment can show that things appear to be unbalanced. But as long as parents are constantly correcting and adjusting, they are probably keeping balance *enough*. And in the end, that may suffice.

Co-Creating a "New" Relationship

In my conversations with parents about their emerging adult children, many of them stressed the importance of seeing the larger picture, of looking beyond one's own identification with one's children. With a wider lens, one is able to acknowledge that talking about one's children is not the same as talking about oneself.

Many parents spoke about the need for guarding against confusing their own issues with those of their children and using their emerging adult children to meet their own unresolved needs.

Parents are not their children. Learning to strip themselves from the identity of their children takes tough, conscious effort. But it is well worth the work. Only then are parents able to co-create new, adult relationships with their grown children. When parents "dis-identify" with their sons and daughters, they stop taking what their children do so personally. They stop seeing their children's decisions as reflections or comments on themselves. With that comes a new respect, a new freedom and a new level of adult communication. Old rules of engagement become less entrenched, leaving space for new boundaries and roles.

Many parents never take the conscious step of dis-identifying with their children and, as a result, their relationships never mature into rich and mutually satisfying ones.

Parenting an emerging adult is a job that can produce a lot of inner turbulence. It often involves holding contradictory feelings toward emerging adult children. The main challenge, I believe, is to express *actively* the loving aspects of the relationship while simultaneously working with the negative feelings. It may sound simplistic, but *let the positive aspects dominate.* It is very easy to let shortcomings that parents see in their emerging adult children—such as lack of career direction or financial immaturity—begin to define the entire relationship in a negative way. Communication then devolves into constant criticism, nagging, sniping and defensiveness. If parents let their positive perceptions of their emerging adults take priority, however, the relationship has room to grow and blossom and the negatives can fix themselves.

Parents of emerging adults are exploring *terra incognito.* It is not that there are no rules; it's that the rules are obsolete. They no longer fit today's realities. For reasons we have mentioned (and for others that we will discuss), it is just not as easy for emerging adults today to jump into adulthood as it was for previous generations. That means parents are likely to remain active parents for longer than ever before. And most are pretty clueless about how to make it work.

Anxiety is inevitable, given the lack of guidance and certainty. However, parents can lessen that anxiety to a large degree when they realize that the vast majority of emerging adults will commit to a mate, have careers and start their own households. They *will* launch. The best thing parents can do to "hurry" the process is *not* to hurry it. If parents can learn to let go of expectations and let grown children be who they are (not who parents want them to be), they are likely to get to a place of adult readiness faster than if parents constantly badger them and send them messages of disapproval, moral judgment and resentment.

A poignant passage by Judith Viorst, author of *Necessary Losses,* provides insight:

> ...although the world is perilous and the lives of children are dangerous to their parents, they still must leave, we still must let them go. Hoping that we have equipped them for their journey. Hoping that they will wear their boots in the snow. Hoping that when they fall down, they can get up again. Hoping.[4]

Parents need to try to put themselves in their children's positions. What would you do if you were an emerging adult in today's economic and social climate? Would you have the answers all worked out?

Chapter 8

SECOND TIME AROUND

Why does it seem that so many emerging adults are returning to the nest after a period of solo flight? Think back to the time you first left home to make a life for yourself. What challenges did you face economically and socially? What roles and attitudes toward leaving home did your parents assume? What messages was society sending you?

Let's look at the "second time around" phenomenon: those emerging adults who return to live in their parents' homes after periods of independence. This may occur after emerging adult children have been away at college, after the breakup of a marriage or long-term relationship or as a result of the inability to make it financially on their own.

The leap from the parental nest has never been easy. This period has been described as "one of the most complex [and challenging] of the chronological life stages."[1] But it has grown substantially more difficult over the last couple of decades, to a degree many parents don't appreciate. Major changes in the global economy have altered the dynamics of independent living. A worldwide economic downturn has upped the ante and intensified many issues. No longer can emerging adults expect to have the financial resources and mobility they anticipated during their adolescent years. Offshore outsourcing and a host of other factors have drastically lowered their value in many professions. Lack of scholarships and grants combined with staggering increases in the cost of higher education have left many saddled with enormous student loan debt. The cost of independent living has skyrocketed, especially in relation to the money most emerging adults earn. Even renting a modest apartment is not doable for many emerging adults on an entry-level salary.

Ambiguity and unpredictability are the rule rather than the exception. Traditional pathways to "success" no longer work. It is important to note that this does not mean that parents are required to accept emerging adults back into their homes anytime they ask, but it does mean that parents should probably view their sons' and daughters' requests to do so with a slightly refocused lens. Holding them to the same rules the parents faced may be unrealistic and shortsighted. The world has changed. It is harder to live independently than it was a few decades ago. The "returning adult child" is now an established cultural phenomenon. Parents can deny it or they can think about how they are going to deal with it if the situation arises. For many, it already has.

What to Expect?

If you have made the decision to allow your emerging adult to move home for a second (or third or fourth) time, you have probably asked yourself many questions related to your role. For example, you may be unclear about what the parameters of financial and emotional support should be for your emerging adult. How do you maintain your own sense of adult freedom when you have been cast in the role of full-time, on-site parent again? Your emerging adult is likely to be unclear about these same parameters. Expectations of each other are probably murky. The revolving door phenomenon brings with it interesting challenges and opportunities. We will focus on techniques, strategies and tools to help you navigate this unexpected new chapter of your parental life. Many of the topics apply equally well to emerging adults who have never left home; however, some of the issues presented are particular to the "returning home" scenario.

Staying Home versus Returning Home

In some ways, the *return* of the emerging adult to the parent's home can be more challenging than if he or she had never left in the first place. Here are some of the challenges:

- You have gotten used to your independence from your emerging adult. You probably don't relish the idea of resuming old parental roles and struggles.

- Your emerging adult has gotten used to his or her independence from you. He or she has matured and changed and may have acquired behaviors that you will find surprising. Your emerging adult may be resistant to your limit setting.

- You may need to readjust privacy patterns, life habits and personal space arrangements.

- You may have to deal with difficult new issues, such as how to address your emerging adult's sexual relationships.

- You may need to consider the influence your returning emerging adult child will have on the younger siblings in your home. Is this going to be a healthy mix?

- Your parent/emerging adult relationship will need new rules. You will need to change the caretaker/child and host/guest dynamic. You will need to make a decision as to how much limit setting is appropriate.

- Your family will need to reinvent itself. Will the returning emerging adult be a part of family activities? To what extent? What financial expectations will you have in this regard?

The return scenario also can provide some benefits:

- The "return" conversations offer a built-in opportunity to renegotiate the rules in a concrete way.
- Your son or daughter may have newfound respect for your rules and privacy, because he or she has been away and is reentering your "turf."
- You will be able to establish new economic expectations (e.g., rent, utilities, food).
- You will be more likely to recognize, respect and honor the maturation your emerging adult has undergone than if your emerging adult never left home.
- You will have broken the enabling patterns of the past. It will be obvious to you if you start to slip back into troublesome patterns.
- You can make a fresh start. The return home offers a real opportunity to create an adult relationship with your son or daughter.
- The financial, emotional and household contributions that your emerging adult provides can offset the inconveniences.

Movies and television sitcoms often paint the returning child syndrome as a uniformly troublesome scenario. Some news magazines report the phenomenon as a social problem. Friends and relatives often judge the situation negatively and moralistically. Add to that the feelings of failure the return home is likely to trigger in both you and your emerging adult—him because he couldn't "make it" on his own; you because you didn't do a "good enough job" as a parent to launch him. It all stacks up to a predisposition to see the return home as a *problem*.

As you consider how to deal with this new chapter in your life, I encourage you to give more attention to the benefits list than the challenges list. Try to focus on the positive aspects and vow to make this "second time around" a growth experience for everyone involved. It is very important to adopt a positive attitude, because the negative aspects are "in your face" in very glaring ways.

I urge you to be more forgiving and accepting. This can easily be a wonderful step toward a great relationship with your emerging adult. It depends on your attitude. Making it work starts by recognizing that you are not alone in this situation, that it is occurring in virtually every neighborhood of every city and town in the United States. According to a study conducted in 2011 by the Pew Research Center, 29 percent of the parents surveyed reported that their emerging adult children returned home to live with them due to the current economic downturn.[2] It is a new reality and not necessarily a failure on anyone's part.

Look at the return as an opportunity rather than a problem.

Coddling versus Support

Here we will be looking at how real families have adjusted to the "second time around" phenomenon and the expert advice of Dr. Michael Bradley, a respected professional who is the author of books such as *Yes, Your Teen is Crazy*. I approached him for advice on the "second time around" phenomenon and I thank him for his valuable feedback and wisdom, which is woven through much of this chapter.[3]

Linda Gordon presented Ben's story and her work with Ben and his parents in "Adultescence: Helping Twentysomethings Leave the Nest" in *Pyschotherapy Networker*.[4] Dr. David Waters, an expert in the field of family therapy, offered his insights on Gordon's case study.

Ben has graduated from college with significant tuition and credit card debt. He is mildly depressed given his current situation: unemployed and having to return to his parents' home.

His parents have decided to help him with his debt. At present they are allowing him to live in their home with few rules and expectations. There is no formal "exit strategy" for Ben, no timeline or set of conditions to be met in order for him and his parents to agree that it is time for him to move on. So he is living at home in a sort of limbo, which isn't making anyone happy. The situation is causing friction in the family, some of it expressed openly, some of it suppressed. Ben and his family are seeking family therapy to help them with this important transition.

What are your thoughts about Ben and his parents? Are they coddling Ben? Should they support him financially and, if so, what considerations should guide their parenting decisions? Dr. Waters believes a certain amount of discomfort is integral to a successful "second time around" experience, otherwise a coddling pattern is likely to take shape:

> I believe that when kids return home…they need to hit a bit of a wall: the situation is different, the rules have changed, and we have to negotiate something substantially different than what we had. It needs to be palpably uncomfortable

and strange for a while, lest everyone slip back into the old way of doing things. I often find myself engineering collisions within families in this situation to get to the underlying question of what the new rules need to be, and magnifying, not easing, the discomfort.[5]

The "second time around" experience is likely to bring a certain amount of discomfort. Otherwise, a coddling pattern is likely to take shape. Coddling reinforces irresponsibility and dependence. When one is coddled, everything is soft, amorphous and relatively painless. Emerging adults have no hard edges from which to push off. Part of the challenge for "second time around" parents is to create enough hard edges—limits, rules, expectations—to give emerging adults the sense that this new arrangement is not free and not without conditions.

At the same time, parents don't want to create so many rules that they stifle emerging adults' autonomy and put their children back into a parent/adolescent relationship. Dr. Bradley thinks it is critically important to consider these issues and others *before* your son or daughter comes back into the home:

Emerging adult children return to the homes of their parents varying in levels of dependency, ranging from asking for financial help to moving back to their old bedrooms and handing over all of their life crises to their parents. There are critical questions that parents should explore with their returning emerging adult child, regardless of the specific issues. The exploration process is key to designing an assistance plan to remedy not just the immediate crisis. This is best done *before* a baggage-laden emerging adult shows up on the doorstep.[6]

I would not always characterize the return home as a "crisis," but I do think Dr. Bradley is correct about parents devising a plan before the move home occurs. Dr. Bradley believes that the success of the emerging adult's second tenure in the family will depend greatly upon how well thought-out the plan is. The danger of not making a plan in advance is that if your emerging adult moves back home first, both he and you are very vulnerable to slipping back into old patterns. In the absence of a firm new set of guidelines, people tend to revert to a "fallback" position that feels familiar. In the case of your emerging adult returning home, this is often a pattern that is more appropriate to adolescence than adulthood.

The pre-return phase, therefore, is delicate and critical. This is where the opportunity presents itself to reinvent the relationship. If that opportunity is not seized, habit is likely to take over and both you and your emerging adult may soon find yourselves mired in old patterns that don't serve either of you. It is much easier to create new behavioral guidelines *before* the move happens than to try to *correct* problem patterns that have already set in.

If you don't seize the opportunity to negotiate new terms with your emerging adult, not only will you fail to encourage your child's growth, but also you may inadvertently trigger a setback. Your son or daughter will experience the return home as another "failure" experience. You are likely to do the same. The result will be widespread negativity within the family.

In order to create a plan that works, Dr. Bradley suggests asking a set of probing questions when the emerging adult is still considering the move back into the parental home.

Returning Home: Questions to Consider

The following questions are designed to stimulate parents' productive thought and discussion. The answers will help to dictate exactly what the return plan should entail.

Before we get to the questions themselves, let's consider two pieces of advice from Dr. Bradley. First, he suggests that parents ask the questions of their emerging adults in a neutral way, without providing any feedback, direction or answers of their own. Parents should ask the questions and then give emerging adults a period of time, at least a few days, to think over their responses. Presenting the questions in written form may work best, particularly if you are prone to steering your emerging adult in a certain direction. However, if you are able to have a mature verbal discussion about these questions without doing too much editorializing, then that can work well too.

The goal is for your emerging adult to think critically about the questions and generate meaningful answers *on his or her own.* That way, your emerging adult will share in the authorship and ownership of the plan from the beginning. There will be authentic "buy-in" rather than the sense that you are imposing your will on the situation.

When asking these questions, parents can offer their own thoughts and suggestions, but only as a last resort. The goal is not to manage children's lives but to give them support and structure in managing their own lives. These questions, framed in the right way, can offer such support, provided parents let emerging adults answer for themselves.

Second, Dr. Bradley points out "these questions must be presented without anger, sarcasm, control, or demand."[7] You need to subtract *your* emotions about your child's return home from the equation. Anger, resentment, criticism and disappointment will not serve the process, no matter how "justified" you may feel in holding these emotions. Your emerging adult is suffering in this process too and very much wants the arrangement to be a success. Again, he probably feels like a failure. Your reinforcement of that perception will do no one any good, so you must carefully avoid the easy temptation to "pile on" to your child's negative and guilty self-perception. Rather, assume that you both desire success. Do everything in your power to create an atmosphere of empowerment, a sense that this plan is going to work and is going to benefit everyone involved.

Ask these questions in a respectful, adult manner that says, "I genuinely value your input."

- **What is the return "mission"?**

  You are probably familiar with the concept of a mission statement in business. Mission statements are sometimes drafted in order to ensure that everyone on the team is behaving purposefully and with the same ultimate goal in mind. Similarly, you should frame a "mission statement" for your son or daughter's return home. What does your emerging adult see as the *purpose* of moving back home? What does she hope to accomplish, specifically? Three meals a day and a warm bed are not sufficient reasons. "The return must be intended as a *temporary* strengthening process, a resilience/asset building program, not a comfortable escape from the stress of an autonomous life," says Dr. Bradley.[8] It should be framed with a clear goal in mind.

  Part of the parents' mission should be to withdraw from their caretaking roles as soon as possible. Part of the emerging adult's mission should be to make a contribution to the household, to use the stay as a means of building personal resources and, eventually, to move on. Write a formal mission statement for the return home and have everyone sign it. This gives the reentry experience more weight and gives everyone a vision to fall back on when things start to get confused and/or conflicted.

- **What got in the way the first time out?**

Very helpful questions to discuss are, "What went wrong during your first attempt at independence? What can we do to fix it?" In business, teams often do a "post mortem" review after a project has been completed. This gives everyone a chance to look at what went wrong and what went right during the process. The prospect of a return home gives your family a similar opportunity. You and your emerging adult can review his or her previous attempt to live independently. You can objectively analyze what worked and what didn't. Looking at Ben's case as an example, we might ask, what led to his failure to find a job and to his incurring credit card debt?

You probably have strong opinions about why your emerging adult's attempt at independence was unsuccessful if this is a relevant issue. You might be eager to zero in on factors such as impulsiveness, unrealistic expectations, underdeveloped resilience and poor decision-making skills. But remember, you are looking for your emerging adult's input. Your son or daughter was the one *doing* the independent living. He or she, in a sense, is the real "expert."

However, your insights are needed too. As Dr. Bradley advises, you may need to look for signs of commonly hidden problems such as depression, eating disorders and drug or alcohol abuse. "Those signs might include weight gain/loss, sleeping too much/too little, loss of significant relationships, loss of employment, moodiness, failure in school, and financial/sexual acting out. Consider requesting a pre-return mental health evaluation for your child if you have any doubts."[9] Serious issues, if ignored or left unaddressed, will likely undermine any return process. Such issues are often harder to deal with once your emerging adult returns home. You are much better off tackling them up front, before behavior patterns in the home become entrenched.

- **How will issues be addressed to ensure success in the next attempt?**

  Once you have identified the issues that may be jeopardizing your emerging adult's independence, you need to work together to develop supports. These could include mental health counseling, financial controls, such as agreeing to bank a certain portion of his or her income, or contractual agreements around problem behaviors, such as setting limits on gambling or sexual relationships while in the home. Any problem issue in your emerging adult's life should be addressed as part of the plan. Remember, though, that the goal should always be to eventually remove any parental controls you are agreeing to assume. Your aim is to encourage independence, not foster long-term dependence on you.

- **What positive steps will be made during the stay?**

  The return home should serve not only as a way of addressing past problems but also as a way of making positive life progress. What career skills does your emerging adult want to learn while in your home? What personal skills will help your emerging adult in his or her quest for independence? Ideally, your emerging adult will use the temporary stay in your home as a way to accomplish goals that would be difficult or impossible to attain while living on his or her own. Getting a graduate degree or completing a technical training program, for instance, might be part of the return plan. This gives a concrete "shape" to the stay, a sense of larger purpose. Counseling, spiritual development, budgeting training or the development of life skills (e.g., cooking, cleaning, shopping) are other positive steps that might be included in the plan.

- **What is the timeline for the return stay?**

  There should be a built-in exit strategy, a finite timeline. If your emerging adult is in crisis right now, then at very minimum you should envision a date by which such a timeline will be established. The timeline should not only contain a calendar date, but also include defined, measurable goals to be completed (and celebrated) along the way. For example: By January 1, I will have a full-time job; by June 1, I will have saved five thousand dollars toward the debt I have accrued; by next Thanksgiving I will be living in my new apartment. It is okay to be flexible and to adjust these dates and goals based on changing circumstances. However, missing goals for "light and transient reasons" ought to be grounds for terminating the arrangement.

- **What will the rules be?**

  For emerging adults moving back home, rules around curfews, sleep/wake hours, rent and chores should be laid out in specific detail. That means using terms such as "midnight" rather than "not too late" and "paid by the first of the month" rather than "paid monthly." You and your emerging adult are likely to have conflicting assumptions that will collide: "Of course my parents won't mind if my boyfriend sleeps in my room with me" versus "Of course

our daughter would never have her boyfriend sleep over."
Specificity will avert many collisions.

A good technique for avoiding endless battles over
rules is for the parents to base the rule rationales on their
own needs and not attempt to lecture emerging adult children on morality issues. For example, you might say: "As
an adult you can decide what your sexual rules and behaviors should be. But we ask that for our sake you not have
sleep-in boyfriends while you are living in our home."

Rules should be respectful and should not infantilize
the emerging adult. However, rules should also be biased
toward making parental dependency a somewhat uncomfortable situation for your emerging adult. The idea is that
living in your home should not feel like an attractive permanent arrangement. There should be costs, in terms of personal freedom, to your son or daughter in staying with you.

• **What happens if the arrangement doesn't work?**

It is important to decide, before your child moves back
in with you, whether you are willing to allow future returns
if he or she fails at independence again. Knowing that they
have no safety net (i.e., they can't go home again) can push
emerging adults to find strength they didn't know they had
on their second journeys away from home. You and your
emerging adult must also be prepared for what will happen if the stay doesn't work out or if he or she is not able
to comply with the plan. Are you prepared to kick him or
her out the door? In most cases it won't come to that, but
there is always the chance that your emerging adult is at a
place where only the most unforgiving response from you
will work. Both you and your emerging adult need to know

that you always hold the eviction card and are willing to play it if need be.

The Value of Discomfort

Overprotection is a common way that things can go awry when loving parents decide to allow their emerging adults back home. One way to avoid the trap of coddling and overprotecting is to agree jointly upon achievable but increasingly challenging short- and long-term goals. In the case of Ben, one goal might be for him to submit five credible job applications per week. But even before he finds a job, he might be required to practice the discipline of going to work by volunteering at a shelter, a school or a hospital several days a week (or even full time). Likely, Ben will soon decide that if he has to show up somewhere every day, he might as well be paid for it.

Underlying such supports must be the explicit understanding that failure to comply will result in Ben's eviction. The message need not be a threatening or negative one; more along the lines of, "We love you too much to see you become totally dependent upon us."[10]

You need to set limits in a way that is consistent with your style of parenting. The tough love approach may not be in your repertoire. But if your parenting style means *never* causing your emerging adult discomfort, you need to reevaluate your approach. Growth, by its very nature, demands a certain amount of unease. If you are not able to look objectively at your emerging adult's skill deficits and help him or her structure an environment that allows for the needed growth to occur, then you should not allow the "second time around" stay to happen. Your acceptance of your emerging adult back into the home must include a willingness to enforce uncomfortable limits when these constraints become appropriate.

Detach from the Results

Don't become overly invested in the outcome of this arrangement. Be prepared for the possibility that your emerging adult may not be ready or willing, at this point in his life, to stick with the plan you have negotiated with him. There may be setbacks. You may be tested. Be ready for this. It is important that you stand your ground in a loving and non-punitive way. It is *your* home, not your emerging adult's. All you ever "owed" your emerging adult was a safe and loving place to live until he reached adulthood. You have already given your emerging adult that.

Allow for the possibility of failure; do not take it personally. The "failure" of this arrangement might be a necessary and important step on his path to adulthood. Do not judge it or assume it to be bad. Change is usually nonlinear and does not occur overnight or in neat, predictable sequences. By not allowing for the possibility of failure, you actually show disrespect for your emerging adult's abilities to rebound.

Reentering the family home includes uncomfortable contradictions. Sometimes your emerging adult will feel like a grownup, sometimes like a child. There is probably no avoiding this. He or she may have earned adult status in some domains and not in others. While economic circumstances may have dictated your emerging adult moving back home, your son or daughter is likely to view him or herself as an adult and will want to be treated accordingly. But sometimes you are still the boss. It's a tricky balance. Elina Furman, author of *Boomerang Nation*, offers words of advice, which parallel that of Dr. Bradley:

- Craft an informal or written agreement that spells out key expectations: what, if anything, your child will contribute to the household, how long he or she expects to stay, savings goals and social rules. (If you don't want your son's girlfriend sleeping over, tell him.)

- Define everyone's role. You are still the parent, but you... are no longer the *caretaker*.

- Discuss the arrangement *before* your emerging adult moves back. Once at home, you have less bargaining power.

- Establish a date to move out. You are more likely to relax if you know [there are goals regarding] leaving, saving and finding a job.

- Have your emerging adult pay rent. [He or she] doesn't have to pay $1,000 a month; even $50 can make the relationship work better.

- Have your emerging adult clean out his/her room. This means getting rid of baseball pennants, dolls and other memorabilia to remind him/her that moving home again is a step forward, not backward.[11]

Having done these things, detach emotionally from the results. It will work out or it won't. Either way, your emerging adult will learn from the experience and will be a step closer to full adulthood.

Finances

A difficult area that is likely to generate friction between emerging adults and their parents is finances (including career choices). One of two of the greatest measures of adulthood is the ability to earn and manage one's own money (the other measure is the

ability to establish and maintain intimate and often sexual relationships). It tends to test understandings of what it means to be
an adult more than any other area. If there is going to be a clash
between an emerging adult and his or her parent during the "second time around," it may well revolve around money.

One question parents and emerging adults will almost inevi-
tably face during the emerging adults' return stay is, "How much
financial support should parents provide?" This was probably
easier to answer in previous years. In the case of "second time
around" emerging adults, however, the financial picture is complicated by the fact that many emerging adults, through no fault
of their own, cannot afford to support themselves. The seemingly
intransigent economic downturn has exacerbated this situation.

Most parents don't have a problem with offering their
emerging adults support when it comes to basic survival needs.
But how far should their financial support extend? For example,
should parents subsidize their emerging adult children when
wonderful opportunities to travel arise? We know that travel can
be broadening and parents naturally want their children to par-
take in these experiences. But to what extent should parents un-
derwrite their children's "non-essential" experiences? Dr. Bradley
weighs in, saying:

> One "life experience" that is clearly more broadening than
> travel is the discipline of denial, of struggling over forced
> choices so that the nature of those things can be fully ap-
> preciated and ultimately savored. If [this emerging adult]
> were living on her own, [it would be] great for her to travel
> abroad as long as she pays for it and then also "pays" for not
> having saved for her future, if that is her choice. Stepping
> in to forbid her use of her own money would be a clear
> boundary violation…

[But since she] is living at home, she should be paying full boarding costs so that her travel is realistically expensive for her. Essentially handing her the money to do everything she wants will only devalue those things and make [her] less able to reason out her future forced choices. She is more likely to think that she can "have it all" and then find that she doesn't have the skills to handle disappointments.[13]

What are your reactions to Dr. Bradley's recommendations? Have you experienced a similar dilemma with your emerging adult?

The Importance of Context

While Dr. Bradley's advice is likely to reinforce fiscal responsibility, his recommendations need to be viewed in context. Personally and clinically, I recommend taking a realistic look at the emerging adult. What is his or her history in terms of money management? What is his work history and work ethic? Has the emerging adult saved any money in the past? If the answer is yes, I suggest exploring the possibility of lending the emerging adult some of the money, with a plan in place for repayment. A frank, open and nonjudgmental discussion may lead the emerging adult to conclude that now is not the best time to travel. Perhaps saving for a trip in the future might be a better solution.

Nearly all parents are conflicted about finances when it comes to their emerging adults. They are less so if they associate an investment with a specific outcome. For example, paying for education is associated with conflict. American parents are more inclined to finance their adult children if they associate the financial support with movement toward autonomy.[14]

Over my years of listening to parents of emerging adults, I have found that at times they confuse financial indulgence with emotional support. Responsibility is best taught by offering emotional support while at the same time requiring fiscal responsibility. This stance is particularly important when things go wrong.

Terri Apter, author of *The Myth of Maturity: What Teenagers Need from Parents to Become Adults*, offers sound advice when it comes to money problems. She suggests that financial arrangements need to be established and understood by all parties involved. When discussing this highly charged topic, it is important to acknowledge the difficulty of negotiating finances in general and to make sure to provide an opportunity for your emerging adult to suggest solutions. Discuss the issues in the spirit of reinforcing your emerging adult's autonomy and sense of mastery.[15]

The spirit of the message is critical. I advise parents to take a non-blaming, respectful stance that encourages problem-solving skills. They need to consider the kind of message they are communicating to their emerging adults. Are they sending the negative message, "You are inadequate" or the more positive one, "How can we resolve this particular issue"?

Changing Expectations: Gina, Emil and Lori

Inviting emerging adult children back into the home requires a willingness to set old expectations aside. Parents must be willing to view their emerging adults as the individuals they are today, not as the individuals the parents have been hoping or wanting their children to be. As long as parents keep measuring emerging adults by outdated factors, they are likely to make their emerging adult children feel inadequate. This will not help them progress toward their goals. The first step may be to try to understand better their worldviews and to ask that they do the same for their parents.

Gina is twenty-three years old and has moved back home to live with her parents, Emil and Lori, and her nineteen-year-old younger sister after dropping out of college. Her parents are struggling economically, since Emil recently lost his job. Gina partied quite a bit during her only year of college and was unable to find a course of study that held her interest. Since dropping out, she has moved from one job to another, frustrated with dead-end job opportunities. The jobs she has held to date do not make her "proud." Her parents are not happy with her lack of progress. Gina stated:

> I don't think my parents understand me and they make judgments about my life. They think I'm moving too slow finding a career and being financially independent. There are too many hopes and expectations and when those expectations aren't met, I feel guilty. My parents don't understand my partying ways and are confused by my behavior. When I meet someone, my intentions are not to hurt anyone. I am about having fun. I make sure that the person knows this up front.
>
> It is difficult, because at times I want to be an adult, but it is difficult assuming the responsibilities of adulthood and living on my own. I feel scared to go out on my own and chart my own path. At the same time, I am eager to know the feeling of being independent, paying my own bills. I guess I want a sense of security, a cushion to fall back on when I slip up. I wish my parents understood what it's like. I lack the confidence that I can make it on my own.

Adulthood is so hard, so many responsibilities. I wish my parents would try to understand me more and look at the progress I have made, despite what I haven't accomplished.

Gina is articulate and speaks poignantly about her concerns. She believes she is a disappointment to her working class parents and this causes her to feel guilt and shame. She is making progress but more slowly than her parents would like. She yearns to be respected for the progress she *has* made.

Gina senses that she is not ready to live on her own, emotionally and financially. What would make her feel ready to be on her own? How can she continue on a path toward independence that would prepare her to "pay her own bills"? Gina feels judged by her parents and knows she is coming up short. She seems to yearn for her parents' respect. Her goals for her own life are perhaps not so different from the goals her parents have for her. And yet she seems stuck, a prisoner of her parents' disappointment.

How can her parents help Gina reach her goals? I strongly believe this question needs to be the focus of their discussions together. A solution-oriented approach would be helpful to Gina, one that does not judge or condemn her. A trained professional may help in facilitating these discussions. Gina's feelings of guilt and shame need to be addressed and diminished. Her progress toward small goals can be acknowledged and celebrated. If that cannot happen within the current living arrangement, then perhaps her return trip home should be brought to an end as soon as possible.

Another route Gina might benefit from is joining a program such as AmeriCorps or the Peace Corps, where she can reflect upon her life and feel productive, responsible and proud while gaining autonomy and self-respect. Dr. Bradley notes that these "real world" experiences can "gift their participants with powerful doses of selflessness, independence, perspective and even wisdom that can build their confidence enough to tackle the next step in their quests for autonomy. Those precious treasures can't be found in an enabling parental home."[16] Going back to college or sharing a residence with roommates might be a more productive choice for Gina at this point in her life. Gina also could avail herself of career counseling services to help her find direction.

Keith's Story

Some emerging adults test the boundaries despite their parents' best efforts. Keith, a twenty-three-year-old recent college graduate, moved back in with his parents. Without a job, Keith had no means of supporting himself financially. After four months of searching for a job in marketing, his college major, Keith's parents asked Keith to find a temporary job to cover his expenses while living at home. He resisted his parents' requests, albeit in a passive-aggressive manner (for example, arriving late to a job interview). After several non-productive exchanges with Keith, it became clear to his parents that they needed to acknowledge that a breach in terms of expectations had occurred and that Keith would need to find an alternative living arrangement by a specified date that was mutually agreed upon.

Given Keith's gregarious and affable style, he was able to find a temporary living arrangement with friends. The new living arrangement facilitated his ability to become more focused and responsible in his job search. He was no longer able to give himself permission to act without a sense of urgency. He recognized that his friends' generosity would be short-lived.

Keith took a temporary job with a well-known food franchise, taking customer orders behind the counter. His personality was well suited for the job and his manager observed his well-honed people skills. Keith was offered a full-time position within six months, with the stated goal of entry into management training within the franchise. Keith had found his niche, although he did not rule out the possibility of returning to his first love, marketing, at a future date. Keith's parents enjoyed the fruits of setting clear boundaries with Keith. Now Keith comes "home" for a comfort-food meal on a regular basis, an activity he and his parents heartily embrace.

Keith's parents understood that they needed to support Keith financially in his transition to the world of work. Co-residence was one way they declared their support. However, they also wisely recognized that perhaps they needed to help Keith in his desire to move toward financial autonomy.

The process of negotiating finances between emerging adults and their parents is not an easy one. It is linked to family values and different ways of being a family. There is no one correct way to resolve how families negotiate finances with their emerging adults. However, the consequences of their actions should be open to observation and discussion.

Structuring a Plan

Many parents are fearful about the choices their emerging adult children are making. Although well-intentioned, parents may act in ways that are counterproductive and sabotage their goals for their emerging adult children. In their attempts to manage their fears, they often control, micromanage or withdraw their affection.

A structured plan for the issues related to "second time around" situations can be effective in getting the relationship headed in the right direction. However, it is important to note that many families can do well with less structure. It depends on the emerging adult child, the family and the needs, resources and personalities of all the players involved. One prescription does not meet the needs of all parents and their emerging adults and conflict is likely to arise from time to time. Whether guidelines are managed formally or informally, *some* guidelines are helpful in order to assist all parties in negotiating a tricky and unpredictable journey.

Chapter 9

CONFLICT AND YOUR EMERGING ADULT

D o you find yourself stuck in the same repeating arguments with your emerging adult? Do you hear yourself saying the same things over and over? Do you negatively entice each other in familiar ways? Do you get stuck on the same unmoving points every time you argue? Do you say hurtful or demeaning things you wish you wouldn't say? Do you both walk away from conversations feeling frustrated, misunderstood and regretful? Do you feel that your exchanges are unproductive and destructive?

Many parents of emerging adults have shared your frustration. Is there anything you can do about it? My research and counseling experience have indicated there are several steps that parents can take with their emerging adults to minimize the eruption of conflict and to defuse disagreements when they occur. Author William James sagely noted, "Whenever you're in conflict with someone, there is one factor that can make the difference between damaging your relationship and deepening it. That factor is attitude."[1]

Conflict between you and your emerging adult is inevitable. After all, you are two different people whose agendas often don't align. But conflict can actually be helpful. It can serve to clarify vague issues in your relationship with your emerging adult child. Unfortunately, if not addressed carefully, it can also leave both of you feeling drained, demeaned and pessimistic about ever moving forward. No one wants a relationship defined by conflict and misunderstanding. Yet very often that is exactly what ends up happening, because people get locked into familiar patterns and won't let go. Much of our next area of focus will be on becoming aware of and consciously altering some of those patterns.

Hang in There

As we begin this exploration, I urge you again to be optimistic. The intensity and frequency of conflict between you and your emerging adult will naturally subside over time.[2] Right now your emerging adult feels a great deal of stress. The developmental demands of establishing a place in society, in relationships and in the working world are conducive to frequent bouts of conflict. As the parent who may be forcing your emerging adult's hand toward making uncomfortable decisions, you are naturally the focus of much of his or her anger and displeasure.

Once your emerging adult feels more comfortable with him or herself and clearer about the present and future, the tides of conflict will ebb. Disagreement will not stop, but its intensity and frequency will almost certainly lessen.

Armed with this reassuring fact, let's see what we can learn about dealing with conflict in the present. Are there ways to make conflict less hurtful, less intense and more productive?

You and your emerging adult can engage in conflict, work through it and both come out feeling intact, connected, heard and respected. You are not required to lapse into destructive patterns that result in the hurling of insults. If managed well, conflict can become a welcome element in your relationship, one that leads both of you toward increased trust, closeness and understanding. The way you navigate conflict can greatly influence the speed at which your emerging adult moves to a place of self-acceptance and autonomy. Once your emerging adult arrives there, he or she will probably no longer feel the need to engage in frequent battles with you. The way you manage conflict can greatly affect its amount and duration.

Getting in the Right Mindset

Before we talk about specific improvements you can make, I'd like you to pause for a few moments and think about past conflict situations with your emerging adult. Replay the disagreements in your mind as clearly as you can. Recall an exchange with your emerging adult that did not go so well.

- How was the topic of disagreement introduced?
- What caused the exchange to spiral downward? What, if anything, led to escalating emotions, name calling, blame or accusations?
- Was there "button pushing" involved for either of you? Which "buttons" and how?
- Did the exchange feel like a "familiar dance" to you?
- Was the conflict resolved or was it just put on hold for another day?
- How did you feel after the exchange? Why?
- How could you have navigated the exchange differently?

Now reflect on a conflict that led to a positive resolution, one in which you moved to a new understanding in your relationship.

- How was the topic of disagreement introduced?
- How was communication handled on both sides?
- Was hurtfulness avoided? If so, how?
- What was it about the way you negotiated the conflict that led to a successful encounter?
- Was there anything surprising about the way the conflict was resolved?
- Did you reach a new level of respect, tolerance, maturity, understanding, communication? If so, how did that come about?
- What role did your son or daughter play in proposing the solution to the problem?

What accounted for the different outcomes in these two scenarios? My guess is that the attitudes and behaviors each of you assumed in your successful encounter were quite different from those in your unsuccessful one. I also suspect that your successful exchange was characterized by one or more of these factors:

- You managed to remain flexible and open, as opposed to entrenched and rigid.
- You felt heard and respected by your emerging adult and vice versa.
- You both contributed to the solution and were able to find common ground.
- You were able to see things from your emerging adult's perspective.
- You managed to set judgment aside, at least partially.
- You came away with increased mutual understanding and self-knowledge.

- You listened more than lectured.

- You grew closer through the exchange, rather than further apart.

- You felt grateful afterwards, knowing that the disagreement was what moved you to a new place.

Identifying the Dance Steps

To understand how conflicts go wrong (and right), the first thing you need to do is to identify the "steps in the dance." When you think about your conflicts with your son or daughter, you will probably notice that they tend to fall into patterns with predictable "dance steps." Some of these steps might be present in your conflicts with other people; some may be particular to conflicts with your emerging adult. Once you learn to identify the habitual steps you engage in and how one step leads to another and triggers predictable reactions and counterreactions, you can begin to re-choreograph the dance.

Awareness is the main key to unraveling the behavior and thought processes. If you really want to change your style of conflict management, you must first develop the habit of watching yourself. The next few times you find yourself spiraling into a familiar pattern of conflict with your emerging adult, observe yourself. You don't need to do anything different, at least for now. Just allow your observing intelligence to step back and watch the "dance" with a measure of objectivity.

Notice the triggers that "set you off." Notice those that set off your emerging adult. Notice the patterns the exchange follows. See where the breakdowns occur.

Later we will talk about how to change the dance; for now you simply need to be aware of it. If possible, solicit the insights and observations of someone you trust or perhaps another family member. Very often, the mere awareness of your own patterns will provide the solution and will tell you what to try differently the next time around.

The goal here is not to eradicate conflict with your emerging adult, but rather to create a process whereby conflict is managed better, in a way that both you and your emerging adult feel heard, acknowledged and respected.

Realistic Expectations

Know from the outset that there are probably longstanding issues that will never change or will change only very slowly. For example, differences in temperamental style are not likely to change. Your "slob" son or daughter may be a "slob" for life; he or she may never meet your standards for cleanliness. A pessimistic child may never become a raving optimist, despite your hopeful lecturing. Acceptance of the other's basic temperamental style and all the positives and negatives that go with it is crucial to finding a conflict management approach that works.

When it comes to analyzing your "conflict dance," perhaps you already know the steps quite well. What you may be unable to do, as of yet, is to insert new steps, such as agreeing to disagree or counting to ten. It is difficult to choose the "conscious path" rather than an emotionally cathartic release, such as shouting or insulting. These reactions may be momentarily gratifying, but in the end, they cause more damage. The conscious path can be enormously rewarding.

Learning to manage conflict does not mean that you always give in to the other side. After all, you are entitled to your perspective, as is your emerging adult. What it does mean is that you give up the short-term gains of emotional release for the long-term gains of better understanding and a more respectful relationship.

Honest differences *can* be acknowledged and less defensive postures *can* be taken. This will allow both of you to forge forward and honor the best in each of you. It all starts by allowing your emerging adult to be different from you. The more that your emerging adult is able to differentiate from you and the greater the clarity and understanding of who he is, the less your emerging adult will be inclined to engage in intense and frequent battles with you. The way you negotiate these arguments can either help or hamper your emerging adult in getting to this point.

Caroline and Alicia Reardon

By learning to recognize the steps in someone else's dance, you may be better able to recognize your own. And in recognizing your steps, I am hopeful that you will come up with alternative choices that work better for your family. It's time to look again at Caroline and her mother Alicia (chapter 1) and gain a deeper understanding of their conflict patterns.

When we were introduced to Caroline and her mother, we had an opportunity to observe how they both contribute to an atmosphere of conflict. Each frustrates the other by adopting hardened positions. Caroline sees herself as an adult, because she has a job and is in graduate school. She believes her mother does not respect her and is constantly second-guessing her decisions, such as her plans to take a trip to Iceland. Consequently, Caroline resorts to lying to her mother.

Caroline's mother frets, because Caroline has not lasted longer than two years at a job. She believes her daughter to be irresponsible and out of touch with reality. Much of her viewpoint arises from the fact that Caroline has not attained the same milestones Alicia had reached at Caroline's age: marriage, children, financial stability. Behind Alicia's worries about her daughter's fiscal "immaturity" lurk fears that Caroline will come running to her when she is unable to make ends meet. Just as Caroline resorts to lying in order to avoid confrontation over her financial decisions, Alicia resorts to nagging in order to head off possible confrontations over Caroline's financial dependence.

Caroline and Alicia each view the world through their respective lenses. Each clings rigidly to her position, convinced that the other is misdirected, misinformed and wrong. Their hardened postures result in frequent arguments and resentments. The tension between them is palpable.

Consider these questions: Is Alicia being overly controlling and living in the past in terms of her expectations for Caroline? Is Caroline a coddled, entitled emerging adult with an unrealistic worldview? Is there hope for their relationship?

New Beliefs Required

I believe Alicia is locked in a nagging pattern with her daughter that is difficult for her to relinquish. Caroline, in turn, is locked in a rebellious, dependent, hostile stance. In reacting to this, Alicia becomes further entrenched in her position and escalates her nagging behavior, guided by the belief that she "cannot let Caroline fail." The more she does this, the more distance Caroline wants to put between them.

Let's discuss how Alicia might come up with new attitudes and behaviors that will disrupt the familiar ones. There are two related *beliefs* that guide Alicia in her dealings with Caroline: "I cannot let Caroline fail" and "Caroline is not in charge of her life; both of us together are in charge of her life." Alicia's unwillingness to allow for the possibility of Caroline's failure keeps her trapped in a suffocating posture. Alicia would feel less constrained and more empowered if she replaced the belief, "I cannot let her fail" with the belief, "Caroline must grow into her own life and choose her own path." This one change might alter the way they relate to one another. Alicia needs to understand that although she is well-intentioned, she inadvertently communicates that Caroline will ruin her life. Caroline obligingly confirms Alicia's worst expectations.

Alicia must redefine potential failure for her daughter as an opportunity to grow, a toughening process that can lead to resilience, rather than a disaster to be avoided. She needs to have faith that even if Caroline does fail, she can and will get through it and emerge stronger on the other side. Her mother needs to tell Caroline that she will provide advice only if requested and that she has faith in Caroline to figure things out on her own. Caroline's mastery of life will come in Caroline's own time, in her own way, and her mother must accept that. Although Caroline may make mistakes along the way, she will also learn life lessons that will be valuable to her in the future.

Presently, Caroline's own set of beliefs fuels the conflict. She believes, for example, "I am entitled to my parents' bailing me out whenever I'm in a financial bind. They're my parents and that's their job." Implicit in this belief is that Alicia is not entitled to focus on her own needs, independent of Caroline. Yes, Caroline can imbibe alcoholic drinks if she wishes; it is her personal choice. But if there is a price attached to that, Caroline must be prepared to pay it. She cannot expect to have her parents bail her out at a moment's notice, essentially serving as her interest-free personal loan officers whenever life doesn't work out as she expects.

It is not clear to what extent Caroline really does expect her parents to bail her out and to what extent that is Alicia's projected belief. But one thing is sure: Caroline cannot have it both ways. If she wishes to be treated as an adult, she needs to manage her financial affairs in a way that does not require bailouts. Substituting the belief, "I am responsible for the consequences of my financial decisions" for her old, dependent belief could alter the interchanges between Caroline and her mother.

Lying's Frustrations

Lying adds a frustrating dimension to many interactions between parents and their emerging adult children. When lying becomes part of interactions between parents and emerging adults, each family member tends to blame the other for it. The emerging adult sees lying as an essential strategy when dealing with a parent who doesn't respect his or her adult decision-making processes. The parent sees the lying as a character flaw and the fault of the emerging adult, a reason not to trust him or her.

Lying creates a self-perpetuating cycle. Caroline has chosen to lie to her mother regarding the financing of the Iceland trip. Caroline's choice to lie sets up a vicious cycle whereby Alicia is less likely to trust her daughter. Trust is a necessary foundation for a mutually respectful relationship. Alicia, in turn, becomes suspicious of Caroline, which triggers Caroline to be even more secretive and to lie more.

A pattern of lying can destroy any hope for an honest adult relationship between two people. Both sides must take responsibility for changing it. Questions of autonomy often underpin lying. Parents need to recognize this. When autonomy questions (who is in charge of my life?) no longer dominate the relationship, emerging adults can move toward a less conflicted stance with their parents, a position that's more like a friendship of "near equals." When this occurs, emerging adults are less likely to lie. They are less prone to defend their positions and more likely to make decisions that genuinely reflect their own choices. In a relationship that is respectful—one that acknowledges differences without heavy judgment—emerging adults are likely to engage more honestly with their parents.

Psychologically controlling parents pressure their children in subtle and not-so-subtle ways. They communicate that they do not respect their children's values and needs. Under these conditions, emerging adult children are more likely to lie.[3] I am not defending lying as a legitimate choice; I am stating that under certain conditions it is much more likely to occur.

Freedom from guilt in the parental relationship is a great marker of an emerging adult's ability to act independently and develop boundaries that propel the relationship in a positive direction.[4] What does freedom from guilt imply? It implies an emerging adult who is comfortable with his choices, who is not directed by others and who is not ridden with fear about disappointing others. The self-directed emerging adult is differentiated from his parents, possesses unique perspectives and worldviews and is less prone to guilt. He or she is less likely to lie.

A less controlling and more accepting atmosphere in the home will eventually lead to less lying. Be aware, however, that removing lying from a relationship may require a lengthy adjustment phase. During this phase, the parent must repeatedly demonstrate that she or he is able to accept the emerging adult's decisions without condemnation, lecturing or judgment. The more your emerging adult is able to see that his or her adult decisions are being respected, the less your emerging adult will feel inclined to lie. This will likely be a slow process of growing trust, not an immediate change.

Parental Controlling

Controlling behavior on the part of parents stifles yearnings for autonomy and results in emerging adults being less in touch with their inner selves. Under controlling conditions, emerging adults have a harder time with commitments, in part due to the fear of failure.[5] They tend to be anxious and indecisive. This touches off yet another vicious cycle: parents become exasperated by their emerging adults' indecisive behavior. They respond by exerting pressure, which is likely to cause or exacerbate existing anxiety within the emerging adult, which leads to more indecisiveness. This, in turn, raises the parents' anxiety level, which increases their tendencies to control.

The important message is that parents are an influencing force, for better or worse. A controlling style of behavior on your part, particularly at this important developmental stage, is counterproductive even if you think you know better. You may *very well* know better. After all, life has taught you lessons. But that is not the point. You need to know that getting decisions right is not necessarily the most important factor. What is important is putting decisions *in the right hands*, that is, your emerging adult's. Giving up control is essential. If asked for directions, you should provide them, but only if asked. Always release the final decision into the hands of your emerging adult.

Alicia automatically resorts to controlling. Her daughter Caroline's "irresponsible" behavior then increases Alicia's anxiety and need to control. The steps her mother takes to control Caroline are maladaptive. Alicia needs to change her belief that she can control Caroline by "stopping her from failing." Only then will Caroline be able to begin the difficult process of examining herself and her motives and actions. I am not blaming Alicia, just pointing out that in her role as parent she can examine her motives, beliefs and behaviors and begin changing the steps in their behavior and attitude. Most likely, Caroline will respond with new moves of her own.

Caroline currently assumes a reactive stance, bypassing the emotional work she needs to do to become a more differentiated, self-aware adult. If both the controlling and the reacting can be removed from this relationship, it can gradually move toward a more egalitarian, trusting situation that more closely approximates a friendship of near equals.

On Blaming

Blaming, like lying, is a trust killer that needs to be overcome before a mutually respectful relationship can blossom between you and your emerging adult. Ask yourself this question: Do you tend to see all the conflict that occurs between you and your emerging adult as his or her fault? The blame game is easy but counterproductive. Harriet Lerner, in *The Dance of Anger: A Woman's Guide to Changing the Patterns of Intimate Relationships,* identifies key traits of "the Blamer," including:

- responds to anxiety with emotional intensity and fighting;
- has a short fuse;
- tends to expend a lot of energy trying to change someone who does not want to change;
- engages in repetitive cycles of fighting that relieve tension but perpetuate the old pattern;
- holds others responsible for own feelings and actions;
- sees others as the obstacle to making changes.[6]

Do these traits remind you of anyone? Alicia? Caroline? You, perhaps?

Alicia tends to blame Caroline for all the difficulties in their relationship and fails to see her own role in their interchanges. Caroline also plays the blame game. So whose job is it to change? Both parties are going to need to make the effort but, in most cases, it's appropriate for the parent to take the lead. Why? As the "senior" and more seasoned party, the parent is in a better position to set the right tone. The parent is the one with the long-standing authority in the relationship and, as hard as it may be to admit as a parent, the parent has contributed to setting its patterns. With that in mind, let's examine the Reardons' interactions further and suggest new strategies and techniques to change the way they relate.

New Strategies

The first thing Alicia needs to do is to make the conscious decision not to respond reflexively when Caroline discusses her plans. This is extremely important. When Caroline announces that she is going on a trip to Iceland, Alicia might try counting to ten in order to give herself a chance to reflect rather than react. Then she could more effectively insert a new, planned reaction, like this:

> Iceland can be a very exciting place to visit, with lots of opportunities for doing many neat things. Caroline, I know I've fallen into the habit of reacting angrily about money matters and I don't want to do that anymore. I'm trying to change my ways and I hope that we can have a more mature relationship that does not shortchange you and your abilities. So I'm going to assume you've worked out the financial aspects of the trip for yourself. I need you to know that I won't be paying for your choices any longer, because

I expect you to assume responsibility for the decisions you make. But I'd love to hear more about what you will be visiting and doing while you are there.

It is amazing how much maturity emerging adults can show when they undertake responsibility for making decisions. Alicia is not "holding the clock still."[7] Rather she is letting her daughter move on in her life and assume the risks, rewards and responsibilities of adult choice-making.

My Own Dances

Let me share a conflict I recently had with my emerging adult son. After making breakfast for himself, he left a slew of pots and pans in the sink for me to wash, knowing that he is expected to clean up after himself. I expressed my annoyance and he claimed there was no dishwashing detergent. In my anxiousness to tidy up, I showed him that while it was true there was very little detergent, there was certainly enough to get the job done. When he made no reply I started brusquely washing the dishes myself.

This is a reaction I fall into easily. My need for order and cleanliness prevents me from being thoughtful about my actions and I automatically step in and do the cleanup work. My son ups the ante, becoming defensive and saying, "Are you calling me incompetent?" I hold back expressing my annoyance, but my posture and facial expression clearly say otherwise. In these interactions, I feel my anger rising. I am not his servant.

What might I do differently to change our interchanges?

In a calm and non-sarcastic voice, I could suggest that if there is not enough detergent he could perhaps go to the store to buy some. (In which case, something tells me he would manage to coax another load out of the existing detergent.) This reaction places appropriate adult expectations on him, without my making judgments about his competence.

Ryan, Joe and Maria Collins's Story

Joe and Maria Collins are the parents of Ryan, a twenty-five-year-old college graduate who majored in philosophy and is currently living at home. He returns home on a revolving-door basis, "crashing" with friends when he needs a respite from his anxious parents. Ryan's attempts to launch himself have been unsuccessful to date. He has had a series of dead-end jobs that have been unfulfilling, tedious and demeaning. Ryan either quits or is fired, after which he returns to the nest to regroup.

Much of the day-to-day parenting becomes Maria's responsibility, because Joe travels frequently for his job. Maria becomes increasingly agitated with Ryan's sedentary lifestyle: sleeping until noon and socializing with friends until the early hours of the morning. She doesn't think that Ryan is accomplishing enough during the day, particularly given his stated goal of finding a job and developing a career path. What typically ensues is a litany of accusations and blame, which just escalates the conflict.

Ryan then takes a job to quell his parents' anxieties as well as to avoid his mother's increased agitation. Eventually he loses the job, because he sees it as pointless, and the cycle repeats. Currently, they are at a place in the cycle where, according to Maria, "He is taking his sweet time organizing his résumé and sending it out." Ryan asserts that he will not take a job that is demeaning to him. All the while, Joe and Maria Collins are supporting Ryan financially during periods of unemployment.

Common Themes, Common Solutions

Both Ryan and Caroline are engaged in nonproductive, repetitive cycles that leave the family members frustrated. In both scenarios, Alicia Reardon and Joe and Maria Collins are doing the same old things, unable to find their ways out of constricting behaviors that don't provide them with opportunities to progress.

As mature adults, parents have a repertoire of skills, many of which are underutilized. They frequently impose rigid steps, rather than taking time to identify negative behaviors and come up with new ones. Again, all it often takes is a pause and a little awareness. Let's see what a new exchange between Ryan and his parents might look like.

At the point that Ryan's mother recognizes her increased agitation, she can recruit her husband's advice to assist her with Ryan, whether or not he is away on a business trip. Using technology (i.e., a phone or text message) she can bring Ryan's father in on the discussion. This may help decrease her agitation, which is partially due to her feeling that she is alone to deal with their emerging adult. Making decisions in an agitated state does not allow Maria Collins's best problem-solving skills to emerge.

As another alternative, Ryan's mother might choose to wait and speak with Ryan upon Joe's return. The conversation might start like this:

> Ryan, I know we've gotten into many arguments about the hours you keep and the efforts you're making to find a decent job. We don't want to get into control struggles with you anymore or to judge you. How you live your life is up to you. But we are unwilling to continue to support you financially at age twenty-five. Do you have suggestions as to how we can find a reasonable solution?

Joe and Maria Collins, by keeping the focus entirely on their own needs, can avoid taking a judgmental or accusatory stance. They can point out that Ryan is welcome to remain in their home, provided he pays rent and participates in running the household. They can tell him that the current arrangement isn't working for them and ask for his suggestions in fixing it. Joe and Maria can ask for Ryan's input as to a date by which he will either move out or start paying rent. They can solicit his ideas about the contributions he would like to make to the household. Without resorting to blaming or labeling him, they can take responsibility for the part they have played in fostering his dependence:

> Ryan, we love you and we've tried to be good parents, but we feel we haven't done the best job in some areas. For one thing, we feel we've helped to create a sense of dependency on us by letting you live here without clear expectations. That's our fault and we want to change it. We're willing to give you a period of adjustment to our new expectations and we're also willing to make the changes on a staggered schedule. But we do expect changes to happen. What would work best for you in terms of a time frame? How can you help us redefine our relationship in a more adult way?

Accepting responsibility for your part in creating the current conditions and keeping the focus on your own needs will go a long way toward defusing conflict and creating a productive two-way conversation. The only requirement is that you have to be willing to give up the needs to be right and to designate your son or daughter wrong.

Are you willing to do that in the service of moving forward?

On Remaining Silent

In speaking of their emerging adult children, I often hear parents share the advice, "You just have to bite your tongue." What does that mean if taken metaphorically?

It suggests a situation in which you are not free to express an opinion and must suppress yourself. It also carries with it a superior attitude, a sense that "I know better, but I'm choosing not to speak." "Biting your tongue" is usually preferable to venting without restraint, which provides a cathartic experience but may hurt and demean the other. "Biting your tongue" is a common but non-helpful metaphor we tend to use.

However, it is still a limit*ed* and limit*ing* reaction.

Frequently at the heart of "biting your tongue" is a message that suggests: "You are wrong, but in the interest of keeping the peace I'm not going to say that." That is the true message underlying your behavior; it is the message that is understood by the receiver.

"Biting your tongue" is very different from exercising restraint, giving yourself time to reflect, listening carefully and trying to see the world from your emerging adult's perspective. What I am recommending is recognizing that you're agitated and taking the time to reflect and think about predictable responses in your exchanges with your son or daughter. Realize that these exchanges will lead to an escalation in conflict and try a different strategy that may lead to alternative responses.

As we discuss this point, I am reminded of an old *Seinfeld* episode in which George Costanza suddenly realized that every instinct he had was wrong. As an experiment, he began pausing in the middle of interactions and asking aloud, "What would George normally do in this situation?" When he identified his usual behavior, he proceeded to do the opposite. His life changed dramatically for the better, at least temporarily. It was funny but instructive. We often fall into classic patterns of self-defeating behavior whereby we keep doing the same things but expecting different results. Consciously adopting a new way of reacting is an antidote to the old negative ones.

So take a time out when you need one. When you hear your internal voice telling you, *I'm going to say something that I will regret, something that will run counter to how I wish to be*, STOP. Pause. Reflect. Remember that the aim is to have your emerging adult child become clearer about *his* point of view, more confident in *his* sense of self and *his* judgment. It is not about selling him on *your* point of view.

Before speaking, ask yourself the question: *Is this a good time to be critical, given what I know about positive relationships?* Along those same lines, here are other considerations to keep in mind, suggested by John Gottman and Nan Silver, authors of *The Seven Principles for Making Marriage Work*:

Being Wrong

According to Gottman and Silver, "One of the most meaningful gifts a parent can give a child is to admit his or her own mistake, to say, 'I was wrong here' or 'I'm sorry.' This is so powerful because it also gives the child permission to make a mistake, to admit having messed up and still be okay. It builds in the forgiveness of self."[8]

Too often in families, there is an unstated mythology that the parents are always right. It is as if parents think that by admitting error they somehow lose their authoritative stature. But no one is right all the time. The need for parents to present themselves as perennially right produces a family culture of distortion, denial and rationalization. Dishonesty becomes the family currency.

Admitting error is one of the most powerful ways to dissolve conflict before it turns into a longstanding issue. It is probably the single most effective way to model good conflict resolution skills to your emerging adult. It creates an atmosphere of trust, safety and fairness. It says to the emerging adult that she or he has a legitimate point of view deserving of respect. It also gives you a "way out" of a conflict that has gone wrong.

Rather than continually distorting reality to preserve the illusion of your rightness, you can instead admit your error and start over. Knowing that you always have this exit is a great relief, not a burden. It signals that it's okay to be human and to screw up, as long as you admit it to everyone, including your emerging adult.

The Magic Ratio

John Gottman also offers this eye-opening discovery about mutually positive adult relationships: The ratio of positive to negative statements is 5:1.[9] Is that the ratio you typically observe?

I have found knowledge of the 5:1 ratio to be very empowering. When my inclination is to be critical with my emerging adult children, I sometimes say to myself, *Is this the one-in-five opportunity I will afford myself for a critical comment? Have I conveyed a positive message in my last five encounters?*

This has worked for me; it allows me to be more reflective in my stance and more deliberate with my feedback. Most of the time, I am able to choose feedback that is confirming and validating rather than critical, just by keeping the ratio in mind. It makes my exchanges with my children a lot less grueling and a bit more fun!

Who Am I Dealing With Today?

Remember, your emerging adult may act like an adult in some ways and a child in other ways. Your emerging adult may change his or her stance from day to day, hour to hour, and you may not know what you are going to encounter when you walk into a room. Conflict may look different on different days, depending on which person shows up (and that goes for you, too).

Keep that in mind when you get into an exchange with your son or daughter. Do not necessarily expect the same "rules" to apply every day. Some days are "regression" days; other days your emerging adult may make unexpected leaps of insight and maturity. Whichever side of your emerging adult you find yourself dealing with, always keep in mind this wisdom from Gottman and Silver: "People can change only if they feel that they are basically liked and accepted as they are. When people feel criticized, disliked, and unappreciated they are unable to change. Instead, they feel under siege and dig in to protect themselves. [Acceptance] is the only approach that works."[10]

Conflict Management Style

It is important to know yourself in terms of your conflict management style. It is equally important to know the style of your son or daughter. Many of the things people take personally in conflicts have nothing to do with them but are merely expressions of the other person's personal style of conflict management, which often differs substantially.

When conflict arises, do you tend to fight harder, pursuing your emerging adult, trying to convince her of your perspective, as Alicia Reardon does? Do you withdraw, responding with righteous indignation? Do you engage in a combination of these tactics, as Maria Collins does? When threatened, do you become more strident or do you become anxious, confused and inarticulate? When you are feeling insecure, are you more likely to engage in blaming behavior?

Your conflict management style may differ from day to day, depending on the context, but it is helpful to identify your general style and the contexts in which your style changes. Do you manage conflict differently at home than at the office? Differently with family as opposed to with friends? What are your "hot buttons"? When and where are you most likely to "go off" without taking time for reflection?

Knowing the way that both you and your emerging adult habitually relate to stress can go a long way to creating a better understanding of why conflicts go wrong and what can be done to correct this. But by being aware of the natural differences in styles, you can anticipate both your reactions and hers. Often you can create a new way of relating, based on mutual respect. Habits or styles can be broken, but first you have to be able to see them clearly.

Tips for Managing Conflict

Here are additional suggestions for working on conflict situations with your emerging adult child:

- Give your son or daughter time and space to vent. Allow him or her to express feelings of anger, hurt and dissatisfaction fully before jumping in to defuse these feelings or defend yourself. Strong emotions are okay, as long as they are expressed respectfully. Don't interrupt your emerging adult's venting with your judgments. Don't try to "fix" negative feelings; just allow them to be expressed and heard.

- Respect his or her privacy. If possible, move the discussion to a private space rather than airing your disputes in front of the whole family or friends and neighbors.

- Use "I" language. Keep your concerns framed in "I" statements, rather than "you" statements; the latter almost always sound accusatory. Say, "I get worried when you're out late with the car and I don't know where you are" as opposed to, "Your irresponsibility with the car is out of control!" Stay focused on *your* needs: "It is important for me to get your rent money by the first, because that is when I make the mortgage payment."

- Don't resort to globalizing. Try to avoid expressions such as "you always…", "you never…" and "every time you…" This kind of language only makes others defensive.

- Avoid "why" questions. This phrasing tends to make others wary, because when people use it, they are not typically seeking information in a genuine way. "Why do you always slam the door?" is not a scientific inquiry. "How" questions tend to be more effective and less inflammatory.

- Listen. Active listening is hard to do, particularly if your emerging adult and you have very different worldviews. Feeling understood is essential to any successful relationship. Listening to your emerging adult will increase the likelihood that meaningful dialogue can occur, dialogue that supports growth and understanding between the two of you.

- Speak calmly. Watch your voice tone and physical energy level. If your emerging adult is getting angry, try to respond as if he or she is talking normally. Don't speak with a patronizing or theatrical level of calm, but make an effort to remain composed. Knowing that you are able to "field" your emerging adult's strong emotions without responding in kind provides him or her a sense of safety.

- Maintain eye contact. As a sign of respect and as a way of maintaining a personal connection, keep respectful but non-aggressive eye contact during an argument (unless cultural considerations dictate otherwise).

- Repeat or summarize what your emerging adult says in your own words. Indicate that you have heard and understood him or her and give him or her opportunities to correct your impressions when the occasion calls for it. Try not to be formulaic in your approach. Your emerging adult will sense if you are being robotic or earnestly trying to understand his or her perspective.

- Recognize the things you don't like in yourself. The traits that most make people react with emotion in others tend to be the traits that they haven't accepted fully in themselves. Often, emerging adults share some of the same traits as their parents and it is these very traits in them that frustrate their parents. When you can understand *why* the vulnerable spots in your psyche are being attacked, you can be more compassionate and less reactive.

- Ask yourself, *Is this really the issue?* Be sure that when you are in a disagreement with your emerging adult you are dealing with the real issue. Small disagreements often camouflage larger issues. Sometimes those larger issues don't even involve the emerging adult but can flow from past pain, from disagreements with parents, bosses, spouses or others. It's not fair to drag emerging adults into parents' personal issues.

- Don't dredge up the past. Keep the focus of the discussion on the present. Don't trot out your emerging adult's history of disappointing you. Don't bring up chains of related "offenses." Stay focused on the one behavior you're discussing at the moment.

- Keep your requests specific, focused and action-oriented. Don't ask for sweeping personality changes, such as "When are you going to start being more responsible?" Be as specific as possible.
- Express gratitude. Thank your emerging adult for his or her willingness to listen and to work with you.

Cultural Conflict: Ina, Amit and Leela Shah

Now that you have had a chance to think about how you handle conflict and ways you might alter your familiar reactions, let's take a look at the story of a particularly challenging conflict between parents and an emerging adult that involves cultural conflict, which adds a complex new dimension.

Culture colors everything, even the perception of whether conflict exists in the family. Culture functions like an iceberg, mostly submerged and out of view, but huge in its effects and implications. There are so many considerations involved when discussing culture that to try to confine the concept of cultural conflict to one sentence would do the subject great injustice.

In one sense, every parent-emerging adult conflict is a cultural conflict. The cultures in question might be generational, immigrant versus native-born American; gender, male versus female; class, working versus privileged; education, college degree versus high school diploma. When people are in conflict, they don't just bring themselves, they bring their respective worlds. Those worlds can clash in ways that go far beyond the personal. In almost every case of people in conflict, there are also worlds in conflict: religions, political affiliations, ethnicities, economic classes, age groups, philosophies, nationalities, teams, professions, genders.

Ina is the twenty-eight-year-old daughter of Amit and Leela Shah, immigrants from India who came to America to make a better life for themselves and their children, who were both adolescents at the time of immigration. Ina is currently working as a high school history teacher. She is outgoing, with an infectious sense of humor that attracts many friends.

In contrast, her parents' social network in the United States is quite limited. Mr. and Mrs. Shah spend the majority of their time working grueling hours in their family restaurant. Any downtime is spent trying to maintain their household.

Problems emerged between Ina and her parents almost immediately upon arriving in the United States. Ina adapted to her new cultural surroundings quickly and welcomed her newfound freedoms. Her parents have held on to their longstanding beliefs and values, beliefs which openly conflict with those held by Ina. For example, Mr. and Mrs. Shah do not believe in discourse and negotiation when it comes to their children. Ina views her parents as old fashioned, restrictive and rigid. She is frustrated by their futile attempts to hold onto the past:

> I have many friends who span the diverse facets of my life. I am very active. I run and engage in fun social activities that allow me not to feel stressed about my financial and personal concerns. I am very good at maintaining long-term relationships.
>
> The more immersed I become in my world, the more different I become from my family. I speak differently and dress differently. When I try to expand my circle of friends, my parents try to tighten the reins. I become rebellious and

push boundaries. Why can't they just go with the flow and be more flexible?

My brother cannot understand my "rebelliousness." He is also pushing limits, but because he is a male it is more acceptable for him and that is not fair. My parents are afraid of the influences that they feel are making me very different from them; they are afraid of losing me.

Ina did well in her studies. She completed college with a major in history. Mr. and Mrs. Shah do not approve of Ina's career choice. In their view, she should become an engineer or doctor, choices they associate with status, income and security. Ina enjoys her job as a high school teacher and feels she is contributing to the world in a positive way. Ina thinks it is essential to find meaning in one's work; she wants to do work that she loves and that benefits others. She thinks that her parents are too materialistic and security oriented. Besides, she does not enjoy the sciences and feels that her talents are more consistent with teaching history.

Amit and Leela have a comfortable, middle-class standard of living, but they work very long hours. In Ina's eyes it is at the expense of family life. Ina is seeking more balance in her life. Mr. and Mrs. Shah expected that Ina would continue to live with them upon graduating from college and that she would move out only when she got married. In an effort not to shame her parents as well as to find an acceptable way to leave home, Ina married an Indian man, whom she divorced within a year. The marriage was "one big mistake." Ina found him too conventional, too "macho" and restrictive. For example, he objected strongly to her going out for drinks with her friends after work.

Currently, the major source of conflict between Ina and her parents revolves around Ina's current boyfriend, Brad, a twenty-nine-year-old artist who is currently unemployed. Mr. and Mrs. Shah feel that Ina's live-in arrangement with Brad is very hurtful. They condemn her choice and believe she has lost her moral bearings. Ina feels that her parents' religious teachings are outmoded and not relevant to her life. She also feels hurt, angry and misunderstood. A part of her, although unexpressed, worries that she may have indeed lost her moral compass.

Ina's outraged voice states, "How dare they question my judgment about Brad? I tried it their way the first time around and it didn't work." In Ina's view, her parents' advice reflects their "old world" view, with old ideas that do not match the times. Ina continues to feel resentful that her brother, who has also been pushing traditional cultural limits, has been treated differently because of his gender and has been given a lot more freedom.

While Ina deeply values her relationship with her parents, there has been longstanding conflict. They argue bitterly. Ina traverses both cultures, that of her parents and the one she has learned living in the United States. This continues to be problematic for her.

Ina's mother and father are disappointed with Ina's choices. They view her as selfish for leading her life on her own terms, which they see as a negative thing. To them, she is dishonoring the family by living with her unemployed artist boyfriend. Mr. and Mrs. Shah feel that she should marry a "professional," someone who could support her financially. Ina accepts the fact that Brad may be unemployed for periods of time and that she will be the only source of support. She feels a love connection with him and she sees that as the primary reason for a relationship.

Questions to Consider

Think about Ina and her parents for a moment and ponder these questions:

- What worlds are in conflict here?
- What are the behaviors in which both sides might be stuck?
- Where are the major blind spots on both sides?
- Who seems to have the broader perspective and why?
- How does the need to be right factor into the prolonged conflict?
- Has there been a genuine attempt to understand, honor and adjust to one another's worlds?
- Where does inflexibility exist among the players and what might be done to change it?
- How are unquestioned assumptions fueling the tensions?
- Is it possible for love and acceptance to exist when the parents' moral system is at odds with the emerging adult's? What might happen if moral judgments were set aside?
- Is it the role of parents to judge the morals of their adult children and vice versa?
- How can traditional values be honored in the face of a changing and sometimes "amoral" world?
- Does culture have a valuable place in one's family heritage? How can such traditions be preserved without choking the future?
- How might a new conversation begin in this family?

Now consider the same set of questions with regard to your own family. Consider the wider perspective of your conflict with your emerging adult. What worlds are in conflict for you? What are your blind spots; your assumptions? Are moral judgments causing problems? If so, what can be done about it? Has the need to be right caused a breakdown in communication? Are there new ways to try to understand and honor one another? How can a different conversation begin for you?

What's the Most Important Thing?

Ultimately, all conflicts lead to the same question: Which is more important: being right or finding a way to work together? Winning or making progress? This is not an easy question, especially when deeply-held religious, moral, political and cultural beliefs come into play. But knowing that this is the *real* question can help you "cut to the chase" and break blockages more easily. Do you truthfully want to move forward or is being right in your position the most important thing? In most cases (but certainly not all), thoughtful parents will conclude that their relationship with their emerging adult children is more important than being right. Only then can the task of healing and communicating begin in earnest.

Being right is vastly overrated. How often does it really lead to happiness? How often does it move relationships forward? How often does it create harmony and cooperation in families? How often does it help solve difficult interpersonal problems?

Parents often get so caught up in "winning" the small battles—washing laundry, dating, music volume, curfews—that they lose sight of the bigger picture. We are supposed to be raising emerging adults who are capable of independent thought and of running their own lives. Is that end served by parents winning every battle and always being right?

It turns out there can be great joy in "losing" some of the battles, both small and large. When a parent finds an emerging adult persuading him or her of the child's position, convincing the parent to look at the issue in a new way, influencing the parent to change habits and perceptions, this is a cause for celebration, not mourning. It means that the emerging adult is finding his or her own voice in the world and learning to get his or her needs met in a mature way.

The End Goal

The end goal of conflicts with your emerging adult is not for one person to emerge victorious but to find a *balance* that works for both of you. By balance I don't mean a compromise where both sides make sullen concessions; I mean a win/win situation where both of you are happier and more satisfied than you were before. This is an achievable goal in most cases. If being right remains of paramount importance, the win/win solution will skitter away from you, always out of reach. Convincing the other of your position is not the critical issue. What *is* critical is structuring an atmosphere where you and your emerging adult are heard, understood and respected. If you are successful in doing this, the intensity and frequency of conflict between you and your emerging adult will subside over time. And you will both grow immensely in the process.

Conflict can be very useful and productive. A difference is declared. Without some degree of conflict, most people don't change or grow. Conflict helps point out problems that need to be addressed and gives individuals opportunities to learn new skills. Conflict helps people to see others' points of view and eases them out of their comfort zones. Conflict makes life more interesting.

The goal is not to eradicate conflict but rather to create a process whereby conflict is resolved in a way that leaves both you and your emerging adult feeling respected and able to grow, both within the relationship and outside of it. The way that parents navigate conflict goes a long way toward determining whether it will be an empowering experience or a squelching one.

Differences between you and your emerging adult will continue to exist. Working those differences through and generating solutions that are mutually beneficial are the keys to the process. Conflict helps your emerging adult differentiate from you. And, interestingly enough, the more differentiated she or he becomes, the less inclined your emerging adult will be to "pick fights" with you. In a healthy relationship, honest differences can be declared and less defensive postures can be assumed. This allows both you and your emerging adult to move forward and build a mature, rewarding relationship together.

Do One Thing Differently

Before we move on I would like to leave you with an important idea based on the work of Bill O'Hanlon, a wonderful therapist and author of the book *Do One Thing Different: Ten Simple Ways to Change Your Life.*[11] It's the simple notion of doing a single thing differently. *Any* change you make that is motivated by love and respect can bring about wonderful and unexpected results. It starts by acknowledging that there is a problem and that the solutions that you have tried before are not working. What can you do differently?

Try to do *one thing* that changes your conflict style:

- Offer praise where you normally offer criticism.
- Try humor if you usually play the heavy.
- If your habit is to yell, count to ten before you say anything.

- If you typically raise your voice, lower it.
- If you find yourself arguing at night when you're tired and at your worst, have discussions at a different time of day.
- If arguments tend to go on and on, use a timer. Give yourself ten minutes and then stop.
- If the language you use tends to trigger a negative response (e.g., for my son, anything that suggests incompetence), choose new words.
- Count your positive versus negative remarks. Stick to the Magic Ratio of 5:1.

Improvise. Change your habitual patterns. Move your relationship with your emerging adult forward.

Chapter 10

WORKING WITH THE GRAIN

Parents frequently become stuck on issues related to control. They don't know when to assume control and when to give it up. Often, parents become caught up in trying to change their emerging adult children in ways that go counter to their natural grain. Happiness, in turn, is in short supply.

Think about your own life. How many sleepless nights have you spent trying to "fix" something in your emerging adult's life, only to realize, with the perspective of time and reflection, that it was not something you needed to worry about, that it was a problem that solved itself or that your emerging adult needed to solve it on his or her own? Emerging adults often become the unwanted recipients of their parents' need to assert control in their own lives.

Sonja Lyubormirsky, in a book titled *The How of Happiness: A Scientific Approach to Getting the Life You Want,* makes a bold statement: Up to 40 percent of happiness is within our control.[1] She further claims that happiness is determined by intentional, deliberate activity. Resilient and happy individuals know how to work the 40 percent, let the rest of it go and live their lives accordingly. They seek experiences that afford them opportunities to change the things that they can and let go of the things they cannot change, not unlike the serenity prayer with which you are probably familiar.

When uncertain times descend, people become particularly vulnerable to seeking control in all the wrong places. They feel increased anxiety about what they can't control and even more urgently try to control what *is* within their purview or what they *imagine* is within their purview, like their emerging adults' lives. How to make the most of the 40 percent that *is* within your control in your relationship with your emerging adult, and to feel at peace with the rest that isn't, will be the focus of this chapter. A byproduct of facing this challenge is that you will probably feel more in control and in charge of your own life.

The Resiliency Lesson

When thinking about the 60 percent that is not within your control, consider: the greater the number of children parents have, the more they subscribe to the notion that children are adaptive and that they will not "break."[2] With experience, parents learn to believe in their children's resilience and in their own. Parents of multiple children are more likely to believe that they have little influence over how their children turn out. It seems that the nature versus nurture debate tilts heavily toward the former the more experienced people become as parents.[3] They take less credit for their children's successes *and* less blame for their sons' and daughters' failures. Experience teaches many parents that their worst fears are usually not realized. In the process, they become more humble about their ability to control and affect their children's destiny.

Your contribution to your emerging adult's development, while very important, is only one of many factors that shape his or her life. Parents of a first child tend to overestimate their contributions. They shift this attitude over time and, by the sixth child, they tend to believe that "the kid is going to turn out pretty much the way the kid is going to turn out."[4] While environment certainly informs who people are, this attitude allows for the possibility of being more relaxed, supportive and self-forgiving in terms of your parenting. It allows for the natural grain of your child to unfold.

Do you need to have six children to learn this lesson? No. It is true that experience teaches us better than anything else, but you are reading this book because you are open to learning about new ways to parent emerging adults. I hope our discussions have helped and will continue to help you to "let go" of some of the control you imagine you need to be exerting. Instead of trying to fix the 60 percent that you can't regulate, try to focus on the 40 percent that is within your control.

Ultimately, the only thing you can control is yourself. None of us can ever really change another human being, at least not directly. Yes, parents can set limits with young children and help them to blossom in healthy ways. But even with small children, parents can't force them to be what they are not. With adult children, all parents can do is change their own words, attitudes and behaviors and invite their sons and daughters to change along with them. Sometimes they accept that invitation; sometimes they don't. If things aren't going the way parents want, they can change their expectations. But the other person always has a choice as to whether he or she is going to accommodate to those new expectations. You cannot change others by force; wise individuals learn along the way to be as comfortable when change doesn't happen as when it does.

As you think of present situations with your emerging adult where you may be feeling stuck and frustrated, ask yourself: Are you trying to control the 60 percent that is not within your "jurisdiction"? The remainder of this chapter focuses on measures you can take to improve your relationship within the 40 percent that you *can* control—the piece that has to do with you.

Optimistic Reminders

Let's quickly review the tips, strategies and reassurances I offered earlier. Your sleepless nights regarding your emerging adult, although understandable, are not necessarily warranted when a long view is taken. Most of your worst fears about your son's or daughter's future will not happen. Few emerging adults, for example, fail to launch. Research shows that today's emerging adults are delaying but not *foregoing* careers, marriage and children. It just seems that they're taking five to ten years longer, on average, to shift toward independence as compared to their parents. However, the choice to follow one's path, a path that might be non-traditional, is an option for an increasing number of emerging adults. Encountering stigma and rejection along the way is no longer a given. Emerging adults are more open and receptive to alternative lifestyles. Remember, though, that in many countries people are *living* ten years longer on average, too. Given the complexity of the world, perhaps it makes sense that these additional ten years be "invested" in the preparatory phase of life, rather than in the retirement years.

By approximately age thirty, most emerging adults *do* settle into careers and commit to long-term relationships. By age thirty-five most emerging adults have their first children.[5] Their aspirations, in fact, closely resemble those of their parents; emerging adults just want to do it in their own time, in their own way. Eventually, nearly all of them secure stable employment, nearly all become financially independent and few live with their parents![6]

Most relationships between emerging adults and their parents improve over time.[7] Tensions ease and communication gets better. While you may currently see your emerging adult as defensive, self-absorbed and irresponsible, your son or daughter will grow up and become a more mature and centered individual. Making mistakes along the way is part of that process. Growth occurs through discomfort, missteps and setbacks. Try to let those mistakes happen. If the consequences of mistakes are dire, step in and do what you can do to help, but then return to your position of giving up control, standing by, letting it be and letting go. Don't blame yourself; actively resist the temptation to view your emerging adult's mistakes as your failings.

Hold on to these encouraging findings, particularly in moments of despair. Your relationship with your emerging adult *will* get better. Waiting may be the only solution. The moment parents truly give up on the idea that they are going to force change on their emerging adults and accept that change will happen on its own schedule, something often shifts almost immediately in the relationship. And parents start to see change happening in the present.

Get into Their Mindset

Making an effort to understand the mindset of your emerging adult is an extremely useful exercise and can help you greatly with separating the 40 percent from the 60 percent. Your son or daughter's life agenda is not the same as yours. While that may be problematic for you, it is not, in all likelihood, something you can control or change. The needs of your emerging adult are bound to be at odds with yours from time to time. You can't command those needs to be different. Your emerging adult ought not to be making the same kinds of choices that you are making.

Choices that feel "reasonable" and comfortable to you might be inappropriate to a person in a more experimental phase of life.

The launching process will more than likely take on a trajectory different from what you initially envisioned. In an article she co-authored with Joshua Hicks titled "Whatever Happened to 'What Might Have Been'?", Laura King proposes that one measure of adulthood is the ability to maturely confront lost goals, lost possible selves.[8] The exploration of "what might have been," the authors suggest, has direct benefits for well-being.

As a parent of an emerging adult, you need to disengage from old goals that have been lost. Before you can disengage, you must fully acknowledge these goals (stated and unstated) and incorporate the sense of loss into your own life story. Recognizing the value of a life that includes painful experiences involves *acceptance* of all the messiness and contradictions. Happiness is not about a perfect life with your emerging adult. It is not without its problems. Struggling with past mistakes can make one feel all the richer for it.

Pain and struggle can be vehicles for growth. In a sense, those who struggle more are given a greater gift than those whose lives are relatively unchallenging. When mature older people look back on their lives, they recognize the emotional seasoning hardships provided and the unexpected opportunities that arose as a result. Hardships and struggles give life its rich flavors and open new doors.

You can help your emerging adult (and yourself) construct stories that propel both of you forward while providing the opportunity and space to explore what might have been. All the while, you can help in moving your emerging adult and yourself toward a story that acknowledges strength in adversity. Then your emerging adult can develop a sense of self that is complex and enriched by *all* experiences, including the experience of loss.

Regret about what might have been is part of the narrative. The goal for you and your emerging adult is to be touched by regret but not defined by it.[9]

Different Mindsets

Journalist Cynthia Broderick insightfully reminds of the life concerns that are on the minds of many emerging adults, including:

- See the world.
- Live in a cool place.
- Take risks with your job.
- Do volunteer work.
- Use this decade to go to extremes.[10]

Most emerging adults want to live life to the fullest and grab the moment. They also want to avoid making some of the same decisions their parents made. They have watched their parents pledge their loyalty, time and life-blood to careers that in their view may have offered their mothers and fathers too little in return. They have seen their parents pursuing material goals on the empty promise that they would bring them inner joy. They have seen their parents' generation make choices that have led to staggering increases in divorce, depression and disillusionment while fulfillment, free time and family togetherness have been compromised. They don't want to make the same mistakes. They want to get it right. To do so, they need time to experiment and to make their own choices that will be clarifying.

This generation of emerging adults is savvy and worldly in many ways. As John Zogby points out in *The Way We'll Be: The Zogby Report on the Transformation of the American Dream,*

Working With the Grain

"...they bite every metaphorical coin they are handed to see if the metal is real or false...Growing up online, they have learned something about the ease with which everything can be counterfeited, including emotion."[11] They value authenticity and flexibility. Many emerging adults still define themselves by what they do. However, for some, their day jobs do not define them. As Zogby notes, they run marathons, play in alternative rock bands, sculpt, kickbox, create websites and blog in their non-work hours. They get body piercings and tattoos even if they work in offices. They have online personas that may be wildly at odds with their work personalities.

An article by Anna Bahney in the *New York Times* further captures the mindset of many emerging adults. A married twenty-eight-year-old concluded that two weeks of vacation was not enough time to lead a balanced life that included the valuing of friendships and family. He decided to quit his job and travel so that he could connect with important people in his life. His wife supported this decision. He made a calculated decision that his skills were in demand and that he would be marketable to another company when he returned from his trip:

> To be unemployed for six weeks is a healthy thing to help you say 'I am not defined by what I do'...It helps to understand who I am, who my wife is, and that our identity is more important than anything we do.[12]

Parents of emerging adults may not be comfortable risking a good job for a reason as "flimsy" as a desire for adventure and friendship. Your emerging adult's mindset may well be different from yours. Can you respect that and still offer your support? That support is still critical. Although they are resilient, the unstable terrain emerging adults are navigating calls for your advocacy and encouragement, not your disapproval and judgment. "When employers come and go, when resumes are patchwork quilts and the workforce largely nomadic, people have to look elsewhere to find out who they really are," says Zogby.[13]

Family provides the anchor and launching pad for many emerging adults, a place from which to explore and navigate an increasingly complex, fluid and challenging global environment. If all you do as a parent is provide that sense of home base, you are giving your emerging adult a tremendous gift.

Why Emerging Adults Need Strong Support

In order to better understand why emerging adults need parents' support, let's take another look at the stresses they face. Emerging adults are coming into adulthood in a completely different context than their parents did. Today's emerging adults grew up with vastly different messages and expectations; they are facing vastly different pressures. And since their parents' generation fed them many of the precepts they've internalized and helped create many of the expectations they carry forth, their parents owe it to them to try to understand the realities they are facing as they move into adulthood.

Emerging adults need to feel that they have something to look forward to. They also need to feel there is a relationship between what they do and what happens to them. Right now, for example, many emerging adults feel there is no relationship between performing well and finding and keeping their jobs. Workforces are now downsized for reasons that have little to do with job performance. Companies no longer feel a need to show loyalty to employees in return for dedication, hard work and creative contributions. Under such conditions, why should emerging adults show loyalty to their companies? Bosses are often frustrated by what they perceive as a "mercenary" attitude on the part of emerging adult employees. But perhaps that attitude is completely appropriate in a job market where caring for employees over the long term is no longer a concern of corporate culture.

Many parents of emerging adults lived their work lives with a comforting sense of having two families—a job family and a home family. That is not an experience shared by emerging adults. And so, the support of the home family is needed more than ever before. It is important to show emerging adults how much parents value them and to offer them the emotional support that is lacking in the workforce. In a time of uncertainty, emerging adults want to be around people who care about them. They appreciate a sense of shared history.

Emerging adults are desperately trying to mesh the optimistic beliefs their parents taught them with the harsh realities they are facing. This is hard work and they value the touchstone that parents can provide. Given that emerging adults are on their own without adequate social supports in place, they are seeking support where they know they will find it. Over 50 percent of emerging adults call their parents daily.[14] Respond to the phone call or the text your son or daughter sends you; engage, offer words of encouragement in whatever communication style to which the two of you have become accustomed. This is not coddling in most cases. You serve a more vital role at this stage in your emerging adult's life than your parents did for you, because there are fewer supports for today's emerging adults. Conditions were already rough for emerging adults in the workforce and they have recently gotten worse. You can offer your emerging adult a sense of comfort and predictability to help offset feelings of hopelessness and despair.

Neither Parents nor Children Can Go It Alone

Emerging adults are being asked to go it alone emotionally, without adequate social support. They are in need of support structures but they may not even know it. Mentoring is in short supply, given that their supervisors frequently find themselves overextended; they are not incentivized for this critical responsibility. Emerging adults may blame themselves, because they are expected to manage all the contradictions on their own.

Society needs to do a better job helping emerging adults make the transition to adulthood. Many emerging adults are dumped from the relatively safe harbor of high school or college into the working world with little realistic preparation. When their belief in unlimited choice smashes head-first into a world of limited opportunities (and the chasm is growing between those who are positioned to fare well in the marketplace and those who are not), many emerging adults are left reeling. High schools and colleges are not doing their fair share of analyzing the marketplace and helping emerging adults navigate their careers. In turn, emerging adults feel rudderless and disconnected and in that state they can make poor choices.

The costs that go along with today's individualistic, sink-or-swim culture are substantial. Eating disorders, substance abuse, clinical depression and anxiety are on the rise. This has been linked, in part, to the lack of structural supports emerging adults are encountering.[15]

Many parents try to fix these problems, but they often require societal interventions as well. Judith Warner, a columnist for the *New York Times* and author of *Perfect Madness: Motherhood in the Age of Anxiety,* notes that a tendency today is to "privatize" problems. Rather than focus on getting society to fix itself, people try to fix themselves individually. The underlying attitude of this approach is a sense of hopelessness. Perhaps people are giving up on the outside world, telling themselves that they're the only ones on whom they can count. Disillusioned by the failure of society's institutions—government, education, religion—to solve problems, individuals have decided that self-control is the only real power they have.[16]

Unfortunately, economic hardships reinforce this point of view. Now people are also questioning once-dependable financial structures, such as the banking and insurance industries. On the plus side, society is at an important juncture where many of the old rules have broken down. People are questioning old assumptions. Opportunity and creativity can thrive in this environment. However, solutions need to be broader in scope and involve all the major stakeholders. A systemic approach is required. Society must make major adjustments and not leave all of the adjusting to the individual. Rather than condemning emerging adults for the choices they are making, parents and society need to examine the choices emerging adults are being offered and ask whether these choices are realistic, given the current social and economic environment.

Society has to do its fair share to help and encourage emerging adults and their parents. We all need to offer one another support as individuals, but we also need to put political pressure where it belongs—on the societal structures that are currently malfunctioning.

Tending to Your 40 Percent

As Sonja Lyubormirsky suggests, resilient adults look for happiness "in the right places."[17] They wisely choose activities and attitudes that sustain their levels of happiness. In the process of trying to gain control of your own 40 percent, look at the next list of behaviors associated with resilience and ask yourself how many of these statements apply to you. Resilient individuals, those who look for happiness "in the right places," exhibit many, if not all, of these:

- They devote a great amount of time to their family and friends, nurturing and enjoying those relationships.
- They are comfortable expressing gratitude for all they have.
- They are often the first to offer helping hands to coworkers and passersby.
- They practice optimism when imagining their futures.
- They savor life's pleasures and try to live in the present moment.
- They make physical exercise a weekly or even daily habit.
- They are deeply committed to lifelong goals and ambitions.[18]

Design a plan for your life that includes looking for happiness "in the right places." This does not have to be elaborate or complex. Which of the activities we've just listed are you most motivated to examine and change? Select that activity and do just one thing differently. After a while, do another.

The great thing about this stage of parenthood is that you can stop parenting your child and start nurturing yourself. And as you do this, you give your emerging adult permission to do the same. You both will feel freer to be who you are.

Going with the Grain

Learn to go with the grain. This is a critical ingredient of good parenting, particularly as it relates to your emerging adult. It helps you focus on what *is* rather than what *is not*. That approach allows the best of your emerging adult to unfold.

What do I mean by going with the grain? To illustrate, I'll ask you to try a simple exercise (though you may need to do it a few times to convince yourself). Lift your right foot off the floor and make clockwise circles. While making the circles, draw the number six in the air with your right hand. Notice what happened? Your foot changed direction.

No matter how hard you try not to redirect your foot, you will probably not be successful. You will be going against the grain. You can think all you want about *why* your foot should go in the direction *you* want it to, but your foot will stubbornly insist upon going the way it is wired to.

This lesson has important implications. A gifted artist who works with wood studies the wood and works to identify its natural grain, recognizing its inherent beauty. The artist works toward embellishing the best of what is already present. Going against the grain would destroy the wood and would result in an inferior sculpture.

In your role as parent, it is your job to recognize the natural grain of your child. Promote and support your son's or daughter's natural tendencies, inclinations and strengths. Build on those strengths. Going counter to the grain only serves to destroy its natural beauty. Put your needs aside and try to see the beauty of the wood. Work with it. Appreciate it. You will feel happier and more in control of yourself and so will your emerging adult.

Do you recall instances where you have gone against the grain when it comes to another person? What was the end result? We have all had multiple opportunities to learn this lesson, but some parents have difficulty applying it to their emerging adults. Parents feel it is their role to decide what emerging adults' grain *should* be. Emerging adults are who they are and attempts to change them are as futile as trying to force your foot to go clockwise when it wants to go the other way.

Think about your relationship with your spouse or significant other. When you first started your life together, you most likely tried to change him or her. Marianne Jaccobi, in a *Boston Globe* article titled "You, Only Different: Why do girlfriends and wives keep trying to change their men?", ponders this process of trying to change "the other." She states that in the past, "I'd overlook…shortfalls or assume he'd change—for the better, for me." With age and maturity, she no longer assumes that this is the case. She observes that her friends who are in successful marriages have learned about what is possible to change and what is not. "These couples let go of trying to change each other…The little things…no longer seem to be a source of irritation. They're little nuisances, endearing even, depending on the mood."[19] I am suggesting that the same is true for your relationship with your emerging adult.

You have learned along the way what you can change in others and what you cannot. Apply these skills to your emerging adult. Stop trying to change who your emerging adult is and stop trying to go against the grain. If you are in doubt about whether you are doing this, ask trusted friends to take a look at the situation. They can often see it more clearly than you can.

Perhaps what makes it particularly difficult when it comes to emerging adults is that they share some of their parents' DNA. On an unspoken level, emerging adult children believe that they should respond to parents' sculpting. Attempt to let go of the idea that just because you are the biological donor you are the designated sculptor of your child's life. Try to go with the grain; when you do, you will find that you and your emerging adult will change each other without even realizing it. Change happens spontaneously when you give up the need to control your emerging adult and let him or her be.

In Eastern society it has long been recognized that whatever one resists, persists; that which is pushed pushes back. So every time parents struggle with one of their children's "negative" traits, they invite those children to dig in their heels and push back. Instead of changing, parents invite those traits to harden. However, if parents celebrate and engage their sons' and daughters' natural strengths, they invite those qualities to blossom. Accept that your emerging adult is not you. Your emerging adult has different talents. He or she will invite different life challenges and solve problems in different ways. Love and cherish that uniqueness; don't try to stomp it out.

Parenting has changed. You may feel it's unfair that you are being asked to remain a parent longer than you "bargained for." However, your child faces different challenges than you did. The time your emerging adult requires to leave the nest may not be the same as yours was. Remember that many in your generation took longer than your parents to launch, too, by adding four or more years of college. Your best approach is to do everything you can to encourage and support your emerging adult's independence, but ease up on the pressure, the anger and the judgment. In that way, your emerging adult will move ahead at an organic speed and you will enjoy the time you have with him or her, even if it is longer than you were expecting.

Each generation faces new challenges and learns new lessons that its parents' generation did not. Choose optimism. Choose to believe that your emerging adult's generation, in the end, is going to be wiser than yours. In the process, emerging adults will be accruing wisdom. They will have to earn that wisdom on their own, however. They can best do that with a lot of support and love from their families.

Have faith in yourself and your emerging adult. Have faith your emerging adult will grow up and figure it out. It just might take longer than you expected!

Notes

Chapter 1:
"I Child-Proofed My House, But They Still Get In"

1. Jeffrey Arnett, "Suffering, Selfish, Slackers? Myths and Reality about Emerging Adults," *Journal of Youth and Adolescence* 36, no. 1 (2007): 23–29.

2. Jeffrey Arnett, "Emerging Adulthood: Understanding the New Way of Coming of Age," in *Emerging Adults in America: Coming of Age in the 21st Century,* eds. Jeffrey Arnett and Jennifer Lynn Tanner (Washington, DC: American Psychological Association, 2006), 1–3.

3. Arnett, "Suffering, Selfish, Slackers?" 25.

4. Jeffrey Arnett, "High Hopes in a Grim World: Emerging Adults' Views of Their Futures and 'Generation X,'" *Youth & Society* 31, no. 3 (2000): 283–285.

5. Arnett, "Suffering, Selfish, Slackers?" 25.

6. Ibid., 27.

7. Ibid.

8. Ibid., 28.

9. Harry Blatterer, *Coming of Age in Times of Uncertainty* (New York: Berghahn Books, 2007), 88.

10. Jeffrey Arnett, "Are College Students Adults? Their conceptions of the Transition to Adulthood," *Journal of Adult Development* 1, no. 4 (1994) 213–224.

11. Larry J. Nelson, Laura M. Padilla-Walker, Jason S. Carroll, Stephanie D. Madsen, Carolyn McNamara Barry and Sarah Badger, "If You Want Me to Treat You Like an Adult, Start Acting Like One!' Comparing the Criteria That Emerging Adults and Their Parents Have for Adulthood," *Journal of Family Psychology* 21, no. 4 (2007): 670–674.

12. Jeffrey Arnett, *Emerging Adulthood: The Winding Road from the Late Teens Through the Twenties* (New York: Oxford University Press, 2004), 15.

13. Jeffrey Arnett, "Learning to Stand Alone: The Contemporary American Transition to Adulthood in Cultural and Historical Context," *Human Development* 41, no. 5–6 (1998): 295–315.

14. Blatterer, *Coming of Age in Times of Uncertainty*, 96.

15. Ibid., 89–90.

16. Ibid., 89–97.

17. Ibid.

18. Bill O'Hanlon and Pat Hudson, *Love Is a Verb: How to Stop Analyzing Your Relationship and Start Making It Great!* (New York: W.W. Norton & Company, 1995), 155.

19. Ibid.

Chapter 2:
Emerging Adults at Work

1. Joel Kotkin, "Are Millennials the Screwed Generation?," *Newsweek* (July 16, 2012, accessed February 2013) http://www.thedailybeast.com/newsweek/2012/07/15/are-millennials-the-screwed-generation.html.

2. Political Calculations, "Are Baby Boomers Stealing Jobs from the Young?" *TownhallFinance.com*, May 12, 2012, accessed July 3, 2012, http://finance.townhall.com/columnists/politicalcalculations/2012/05/12/are_baby_boomers_stealing_jobs_from_the_young_part_1.

3. Jeffrey Arnett, "Suffering, Selfish, Slackers? Myths and Reality about Emerging Adults," *Journal of Youth and Adolescence*, 36, no. 1 (2007): 28.

4. Ibid.

5. Harry Blatterer, *Coming of Age in Times of Uncertainty* (New York: Berghahn Books, 2007), 89–97.

6. Jean M. Twenge, *Generation Me: Why Today's Young Americans Are More Confident, Assertive, Entitled— and More Miserable Than Ever Before* (New York, NY: Free Press, 2006), 109.

7. Dianne M. Durkin, *The Loyalty Advantage: Essential Steps to Energize Your Company, Your Customers, Your Brand* (New York: AMACOM, 2005), 34.

8. Christine Hassler, *20-Something, 20-Everything: A Quarter-Life Woman's Guide to Balance and Direction* (Novato, CA: New World Library, 2005), 274–276; Christine Hassler, *20 Something Manifesto: Quarter-Lifers Speak Out About Who They Are, What They Want, and How to Get It* (Novato, CA: New World Library, 2008), 232.

9. Hassler, *20-Something, 20-Everything*, 275.

10. Ibid., 273.

11. Ibid., 272.

12. Rich W. Feller, Stevie L. Honaker and Lynn M. Zagzebski, "Theoretical Voices Directing the Career Development Journey: Holland, Harris-Bowlsbey, and Krumboltz," *Career Development Quarterly* 49, no. 3 (2001): 215.

13. Varda Konstam and Ilana Lehmann, "Emerging Adults at Work and at Play: Leisure, Work Engagement, and Career Indecision," *Journal of Career Assessment* 19, no. 2 (2011): 151–164.

14. Merle Johnson, ed., *More Maxims of Mark* (New York: Privately published, 1927), 14.

15. Jessica Godofsky, Cliff Zukin and Carl Van Horn, "Unfulfilled Expectations: Recent College Graduates Struggle in a Troubled Economy," *Worktrends: Americans' Attitudes About Work, Employers, and Government,* May 2011, accessed March 24, 2012, http://www.heldrich.rutgers.edu/sites/default/files/content/Work_Trends_May_2011.pdf.

16. Ulla Hytti, "From Unemployment to Entrepreneurship: Constructing Different Meanings" (paper presented in the Rent XVII Workshop, Lodz, Poland, November 20-21, 2003), accessed November 11, 2012, http://130.203.133.150/viewdoc/download?doi=10.1.1.200 .9544&rep=rep1&type=pdf; Matsidiso N. Naong, "Promotion of Entrepreneurship Education—A Remedy to Graduates and Youth Unemployment—A Theoretical Perspective," *Journal of Social Sciences* 28, no. 3 (2011): 187.

17. Arnold Kling and Nick Schulz, "Solving the Long-Term Jobs Problem," *The American*, July 27, 2011, accessed November 10, 2012, http://www.american.com/archive/2011/july/solving-the-long-term -jobs-problem.

Chapter 3:
Career Indecision or Experimentation?

1. John Bynner, Elsa Ferri and Peter Shepherd, eds., *Twenty-Something in the 1990s: Getting On, Getting By, Getting Nowhere* (Surrey, UK: Ashgate Publishing, 1997), 119–128, quoted in European Group for Integrated Social Research, "Misleading Trajectories: Transition Dilemmas of Young Adults in Europe," *Journal of Youth Studies* 4, no. 1 (2001): 103–104.

2. Barry Schwartz, *The Paradox of Choice: Why More is Less* (New York, NY: Harper Perennial, 2004).

3. Itamar Gati, Lisa Asulin-Peretz and Ahinoam Fisher, "Emotional and Personality-Related Career Decision-Making Difficulties: A 3-Year Follow-Up," *The Counseling Psychologist* 40, no. 1 (2011): 7.

4. Judy M. Chartrand, Melissa L. Rose, Timothy R. Elliott, Cheri Marmarosh and Susan Caldwell, "Peeling Back the Onion: Personality, Problem Solving, and Career Decision-Making Style Correlates of Career Indecision," *Journal of Career Assessment* 1, no. 1 (1993): 69, quoted in Itamar Gati, Lisa Asulin-Peretz and Ahinoam Fisher, "Emotional and Personality-Related Career Decision-Making Difficulties: A 3-Year Follow-Up," *The Counseling Psychologist* 40, no. 1 (2011): 7.

5. Bureau of Labor Statistics, "America's Young Adults at 24: School Enrollment, Training, and Employment Transitions Between Ages 23 and 24," U.S. Department of Labor, February 9, 2012, accessed July 24, 2012, http://www.bls.gov/news.release/pdf/nlsyth.pdf.

6. Shmuel Shulman, Sidney J. Blatt and Benni Feldman, "Vicissitudes of the Impetus for Growth and Change among Emerging Adults," *Psychoanalytic Psychology* 23 (2006): 164.

7. Donald E. Super, *The Psychology of Careers: An Introduction to Vocational Development* (New York, NY: Harper, 1957); Donald E. Super, "A Life-Span, Life-Space Approach to Career Development," in *Career Choice and Development: Applying Contemporary Theories to Practice,* edited by Duane Brown and Linda Brooks (San Francisco, CA: Jossey-Bass, 1990): 197–261.

8. Super, "A Life-Span, Life-Space Approach to Career Development."

9. Paul R. Salomone, "Difficult Cases in Career Counseling: II. The Indecisive Client," *Personnel and Guidance Journal* 60, no. 8 (1982): 499.

10. Ibid., 497–498.

11. Varda Konstam and Ilana Lehmann, "Emerging Adults at Work and at Play: Leisure, Work Engagement, and Career Indecision," *Journal of Career Assessment* 19, no. 2 (2011): 151–164.

12. Kevin R. Kelly and Wei-Chien Lee, "Mapping the Domain of Career Decision Problems," *Journal of Vocational Behavior* 61, no. 2 (2002): 302–326.

13. Ibid., 322.

14. Ilana Lehmann and Varda Konstam, "Growing up Perfect: Perfectionism, Problematic Internet Use, and Career Indecision in Emerging Adults," *Journal of Counseling and Development* 89, no. 2 (2011): 155–162.

15. Daniel C. Feldman, "The Antecedents and Consequences of Early Career Indecision among Young Adults," *Human Resource Management Review* 13, no. 3 (2003): 526.

16. Schwartz, *The Paradox of Choice*, 9–18.

17. Dan Ariely, *Predictably Irrational: The Hidden Forces that Shape Our Decisions* (New York, NY: HarperCollins, 2008), 142.

220

Notes

18. John Tierney, "The Advantages of Closing a Few Doors," *New York Times*, February 26, 2008, accessed January 12, 2012, http://www.nytimes.com/2008/02/26/science/26tier.html?_r=1&oref=slogin.

19. Ariely, *Predictably Irrational,* 149–150.

20. Ibid., 151.

Chapter 4:
From the Professional to the Personal

1. Robert Schoen, Nancy S. Lansdale, and Kimberly Daniels, "Family Transitions in Young Adulthood," *Demography* 44 (2007): 817–818.

2. Paula Y. Goodwin, William D. Mosher and Anjani Chandra, "Marriage and Cohabitation in the United States: A statistical portrait based on Cycle 6 (2002) of the National Survey of Family Growth," *Vital Health Statistics* 23, no. 28 (2010) http://www.cdc.gov/nchs/data/series/sr_23/sr23_028.pdf.

3. Scott M. Stanley, Galena Kline Rhoades and Howard J. Markman, "Sliding Versus Deciding: Inertia and the Premarital Cohabitation Effect," *Family Relations* 55, no. 4 (2006): 500.

4. Varda Konstam, *Emerging and Young Adulthood: Multiple Perspectives, Diverse Narratives* (New York, NY: Springer Press, 2007), 68.

5. Ibid., 69.

6. Ethan Watters, "In My Tribe," in *Before the Mortgage: Real Stories of Brazen Loves, Broken Leases, and the Perplexing Pursuit of Adulthood,* edited by Christina Amini and Rachel Hutton (New York, NY: Simon Spotlight Entertainment, 2006): 88.

7. Ibid., 88–89.

8. Varda Konstam, Ilana Lehmann and Sarah Tomek, "Friends We Have Never Met: Pathways in Emerging Adults" (Preprint submitted September 5, 2012).

9. Darius K.-S. Chan and Grand H.-L. Cheng, "A Comparison of Offline and Online Friendship Qualities at Different Stages of Relationship Development," *Journal of Social and Personal Relationships* 21, no. 3 (2004): 316, doi: 10.1177/0265407504042834.

10. Konstam, *Emerging and Young Adulthood,* 64.

11. Mark R. Fondacaro and Kenneth Heller, "Social Support Factors and Drinking among College Student Males," *Journal of Youth and Adolescence* 12, no. 4 (1983): 285–299, quoted in Michael Kimmel, *Guyland: The Perilous World Where Boys Become Men* (New York, NY: HarperCollins, 2008), 107.

12. Michael Kimmel, *Guyland: The Perilous World Where Boys Become Men* (New York, NY: HarperCollins, 2008), 109.

13. Hara Estroff Marano, *A Nation of Wimps: The High Cost of Invasive Parenting* (New York, NY: Broadway Books, 2008), 153.

14. Jennifer R. Boyle and Bradley O. Boekeloo, "Perceived Parental Approval of Drinking and Its Impact on Problem Drinking Behaviors Among First-Year College Students," *Journal of American College Health* 54, no. 4 (2006): 240.

15. Bruce D. Bartholow, Kenneth J. Sher and Jennifer L. Krull, "Changes in Heavy Drinking Over the Third Decade of Life As a Function of Collegiate Fraternity and Sorority Involvement: A Prospective, Multilevel Analysis," *Health Psychology* 22, no. 6 (2003): 616–626.

16. Ibid., 624.

17. E. Mavis Hetherington and Margaret Stanley-Hagan, "The Adjustment of Children with Divorced Parents: A Risk and Resiliency Perspective," *Journal of Clinical Psychology and Psychiatry* 40, no. 1 (1999): 130; Dorit Eldar-Avidan, Muhammed M. Haj-Yahia and Charles W. Greenbaum, "Divorce Is a Part of My Life. Resilience, Survival, and Vulnerability: Young Adults' Perception of the Implications of Parental Divorce," *Journal of Marital and Family Therapy* 35, no. 1 (2009): 41.

18. Ming Cui, Frank D. Fincham and B. Kay Pasley, "Young Adult Romantic Relationships: The Role of Parents' Marital Problems and Relationship Efficacy," *Personality and Social Psychology Bulletin* 34, no. 9 (2008): 1233.

19. Judith S. Wallerstein and Julia M. Lewis, "The Unexpected Legacy of Divorce: Report of a 25- Year Study," *Psychoanalytic Psychology* 21, no. 3 (2004): 368.

20. Varda Konstam, "Emerging Adults and Parental Divorce: Coming to Terms with 'What Might Have Been,'" *Journal of Systemic Therapies* 28, no. 4 (2009): 29.

21. Laura A. King and Courtney Raspin, "Lost and Found Possible Selves, Subjective Well-Being, and Ego Development in Divorced Women," *Journal of Personality* 72, no. 3 (2004): 627.

22. Jennifer L. Tanner, Jeffrey Jensen Arnett and Julie A. Leis, "Emerging Adulthood: Learning and Development During the First Stage of Adulthood," in *Handbook of Research on Adult Development and Learning*, edited by M. Cecil Smith with Nancy DeFrates-Densch (New York, NY: Taylor & Francis, 2009), 52–53.

23. Alison Lobron, "Meet. Marry. Move On," *Boston Globe*, July 15, 2007, accessed November 10, 2012. http://www.boston.com/news/globe/magazine/articles/2007/07/15/meet_marry_move_on/?page=full.

Chapter 5:
Technology in the Lives of Emerging Adults

1. Michelle Slatalla, "Dear Stranger: It's 4 a.m. Help. Cyberfamilia," *New York Times,* (August 2008, E2.)

2. Matt Richtell, "Don't Want to Talk about It? Order a Missed Call," *New York Times* (August 2008, A1, 12.)

3. Personal communication with Dr. Wayne Weiner, December 2, 2011.

4. Kate E. Jackson, "Look homeward, Generation X," *Sunday Boston Globe* (March 2008, H1, H4.)

5. Patricia Wallace, *The Psychology of the Internet* (UK: Cambride University Press, 1999), 9.

6. Ibid., 132, 202.

7. U.S. Department of Education, Office of Planning, Evaluation and Policy Development, Policy and Program Studies Service, *Analysis of State Bullying Laws and Policies*, Washington, D.C. 2011, 127-129.

8. Katelyn Y. A. McKenna and John A. Bargh, "Coming Out in The Age of the Internet: Identity "Demarginalization" through Virtual Group Participation," *Journal of Personality and Social Psychology* 75, 3(1998), 692.

9. Ashlee Vance, "Facebook: The Making of 1 Billion Users," *Bloomberg Business Week Technology*, (October 2012, accessed November 2012) http://www.businessweek.com/articles/2012-10-04/facebook-the-making-of-1-billion-users.

10. Alice Mathias, "The Facebook Generation," *New York Times* (October 2007, accessed June 2012) http://www.nytimes.com/2007/10/06/opinion/06mathias.html.

11. Ibid.

12. Stephanie Rosenbloom, "Putting Your Best Cyberface Forward," *New York Times* (January 3, 2008, accessed October 2012) http://www.nytimes.com/2008/01/03/fashion/03impression.html?pagewanted=all&_r=0.

13. Personal communication with Dr. Rick Houser, March 4, 2011.

14. Ilana S. Lehmann and Varda Konstam, "Twitter, Personality and Friendships," Preprint submitted (December 12, 2012)

15. Oliver P. John, E.M. Donahue and R. L. Kentle "The Big Five Inventory—Versions 4a and 54." (Berkeley, CA: University of California, Berkeley, Institute of Personality and Social Research. 1991)

16. Norman H. Nie and Lutz Erbring, "Internet and Society: A Preliminary Report," (February 2000, accessed October 2012) http://www.bsos.umd.edu/socy/alan/webuse/handouts/Nie%20and%20Erbring-Internet%20and%20Society%20a%20Preliminary%20Report.pdf.

17. Ibid.

18. Ethan Gilsdorf, "My Escape to the Dungeon," *The Boston Globe* (March 2008, A11)

19. Ibid.

20. Kimberly S. Young, Xiao D. Yue, and Li Ying, "Prevalence Estimates and Etiologic Models of Internet Addiction," in *Internet Addiction: A Handbook and Guide to Evaluation and Treatment,* ed. Kimberly S. Young and Christiano N. de Abreu (Hoboken, NJ: John Wiley & Sons, 2011), 5–6.

21. Sandra Ramussen, *Addiction Treatment: Theory and Practice* (London: Sage Publications 2000) 86

22. Kimberly S. Young, *Caught in the Net: How to Recognize the Signs of Internet Addiction and A Winning Strategy for Recovery* (New York: John Wiley, 1998), 3–4.

23. Personal communication with Dr. Rick Houser, March 4, 2011.

24. Kimberly S. Young, "Internet Addiction: The Emergence Of A New Clinical Disorder" (paper presented at the 104th annual meeting of the American Psychological Association, Toronto, Canada, August 15, 1996).

25. Jeffrey Michael Parsons. "An examination of massively multiplayer on-line role-playing games as a facilitator of internet addiction." (University of Iowa, 2005.) http://ir.uiowa.edu/etd/98.

26. Richard Foreman, "The Pancake People, Or, "the Gods Are Pounding My Head," *Edge* (March 2005, accessed May 2012) http://www.edge .org/3rd_culture/foreman05/foreman05_index.html.

27. Mark Bittman, "I Need a Virtual Break. No, Really," *New York Times* (March 2008) 1, 14.

28. Joel Garreau, "Friends Indeed? As We Click With More Pals Online, The Idea of Friendship Multiplies," *The Washington Post* (April 2008) M1, M6.

Chapter 6:
Parenting an Emerging Adult

1. William S. Aquilino, "Family Relationships and Support Systems in Emerging Adulthood" quoted in *Emerging Adults in America: Coming of Age in the 21st Century*, edited by Jeffrey Jensen Arnett and Jennifer Lynn Tanner (Washington, DC: American Psychological Association, 2005), 193–217.

2. Wendy S. White, "Students, Parents, Colleges: Drawing the Lines," *Chronicle of Higher Education* 52, no. 17 (2005).

3. Sue Shellenbarger, "Tucking the Kids In—in the Dorm: Colleges Ward Off Overinvolved Parents," *Wall Street Journal*, July 28, 2005, accessed March 15, 2012, http://online.wsj.com/article/ 0,,SB112250452603298007,00.html.

4. Madeline Levine, *The Price of Privilege: How Parental Pressure and Material Advantage Are Creating a Generation of Disconnected and Unhappy Kids* (New York, NY: Harper, 2006), 10–11.

5. Aquilino, "Family Relationships and Support Systems in Emerging Adulthood," 193–217.

6. William S. Aquilino, "From Adolescent to Young Adult: A Prospective Study of Parent-Child Relations during the Transition to Adulthood," *Journal of Marriage and the Family* 59, no. 3 (1997): 683.

7. Levine, *The Price of Privilege,* 70.

8. Paul Taylor, Gretchen Livingston, Kim Parker, Wendy Wang and Daniel Dockterman, "Since the Start of the Great Recession, More Children Raised by Grandparents," *Pew Research Center's Social & Demographic Trends Project,* September 9, 2010, accessed November 10, 2012, http://www.pewsocialtrends.org/files/2010/10/764-children-raised-by-grandparents.pdf.

9. Gillian Douglas and Neil Ferguson, "The Role of Grandparents in Divorced Families," *International Journal of Law, Policy and the Family* 17, no. 1 (2003), 42.

10. Taylor, et al., "Since the Start of the Great Recession," 4.

11. Douglas and Ferguson, "The Role of Grandparents in Divorced Families," 61–62.

12. Tamar Lewin, "Child's Education, but Parents' Crushing Loans," *New York Times,* November 11, 2012, accessed November 12, 2012, http://www.nytimes.com/2012/11/12/business/some-parents-shouldering-student-loans-fall-on-tough-times.html?pagewanted=all&_r=0.

13. Kim Parker, "The Boomerang Generation: Feeling OK about Living with Mom and Dad," *Pew Social & Demographic Trends,* March 15, 2012, accessed June 24, 2012, http://www.pewsocialtrends.org/files/2012/03/PewSocialTrends-2012-BoomerangGeneration.pdf.

14. Rubén G. Rumbaut, "Young Adults in the United States: A Profile," *Research Network Working Paper No. 4* (2004): 6, accessed July 20, 2012, http://papers.ssrn.com/sol3/papers.cfm?abstract_id=1887827.

15. Ibid.

16. Paul Taylor, Kim Parker, Rakesh Kochhar, Richard Fry, Cary Funk, Eileen Patten and Seth Motel, "Young, Underemployed and Optimistic: Coming of Age, Slowly, in a Tough Economy," *Pew Social & Demographic Trends,* February 9, 2012, accessed April 6, 2012, http://www.pewsocialtrends.org/files/2012/02/young-underemployed-and-optimistic.pdf.

Chapter 7:
Standing By, Letting It Be and Letting Go

1. Sharon Jayson, "Many 'emerging adults' 18–29 are not there yet," *USA Today*, July 30, 2012, accessed August 15, 2012, http://www.usatoday.com/news/health/wellness/story/2012-07-30/Emerging-adults-18-29-still-attached-to-parents/56575404/1.

2. Bill O'Hanlon, *Do One Thing Different: Ten Simple Ways to Change Your Life* (New York, NY: HarperCollins, 1999), 180.

3. Karen Levin Coburn and Madge Lawrence Treeger, *Letting Go: A Parents' Guide to Understanding the College Years*, 4th ed. (New York: HarperCollins, 2003), 210.

4. Judith Viorst, *Necessary Losses: The Loves, Illusions, Dependencies, and Impossible Expectations That All of Us Have to Give Up in Order to Grow* (New York, NY: Fireside, 1998), 222.

Chapter 8:
Second Time Around

1. Jennifer Tanner and Scott Yabiku, "Conclusion: The Economics of Young Adulthood—One Future or Two?" in *Transitions to Adulthood in a Changing Economy: No Work, No Family, No Future?* edited by Alan Booth, Ann C. Crouter and Michael Shanahan (Westport, CT: Praeger Publishers, 1999), 257.

2. Kim Parker, "The Boomerang Generation: Feeling OK about Living with Mom and Dad," *Pew Social & Demographic Trends*, March 15, 2012, accessed May 23, 2012, http://www.pewsocialtrends.org/files/2012/03/PewSocialTrends-2012-BoomerangGeneration.pdf.

3. Michael Bradley, e-mail message to the author, August 28, 2012.

4. Linda Gordon, "Adultescence: Helping twentysomethings leave the nest," *Psychotherapy Networker* 29, no. 2 (2005): 74–76.

5. Ibid., 76.

6. Bradley, e-mail message to the author.

7. Ibid.

8. Ibid.

9. Ibid.

10. Ibid.

11. Elina Furman, *Boomerang Nation: How to Survive Living with Your Parents...the Second Time Around* (New York, NY: Fireside, 2005).

12. Varda Konstam, *Emerging and Young Adulthood: Multiple Perspectives, Diverse Narratives* (New York, NY: Springer Press, 2007), 98.

13. Bradley, e-mail message to the author.

14. William S. Aquilino, "Family Relationships and Support Systems in Emerging Adulthood," quoted in *Emerging Adults in America: Coming of Age in the 21st Century*, edited by Jeffrey Jensen Arnett and Jennifer Lynn Tanner (Washington, DC: American Psychological Association, 2006), 204.

15. Terri Apter, *The Myth of Maturity: What Teenagers Need from Parents to Become Adults* (New York, NY: W. W. Norton & Company, Inc., 2001), 224–237.

16. Bradley, e-mail message to the author.

Chapter 9:
Conflict and Your Emerging Adult

1. William James, *Goodreads.com*, accessed May 2012, http://www.goodreads.com/author/quotes/15865.William_James.

2. Lene Arnett Jensen, Jeffery Jensen Arnett, S. Shirley Feldman and Elizabeth Cauffman, "The Right to Do Wrong: Lying to Parents among Adolescents and Emerging Adults," *Journal of Youth and Adolescence*, 33, no. 2 (2004), 102.

3. Ibid.

4. Schmuel Shulman and Inge Seiffge-Krenke, *Fathers and Adolescents: Developmental and Clinical Perspectives* (London, UK: Routledge, 1997), 224.

5. Koen Luyckx, Maarten Vansteenkiste, Luc Goossens and Michael D. Berzonsky, "Parental Psychological Control and Dimensions of Identity Formation in Emerging Adulthood," *Journal of Family Psychology* 21, no. 21 (2007): 547.

6. Harriet Lerner, *The Dance of Anger: A Woman's Guide to Changing the Patterns of Intimate Relationships* (New York, NY: HarperCollins, 1985), 192–193.

7. Ibid., 214.

8. John Gottman and Nan Silver, *The Seven Principles for Making Marriage Work: A Practical Guide from the Country's Foremost Relationship Expert* (New York, NY: Three Rivers Press, 1999), 149.

9. John M. Gottman, *What Predicts Divorce? The Relationship Between Marital Processes and Marital Outcomes* (Hillsdale, NJ: Lawrence Erlbaum Associates, Inc., 1994), 183.

10. Gottman and Silver, *The Seven Principles for Making Marriage Work,* 149.

11. Bill O'Hanlon, *Do One Thing Different: Ten Simple Ways to Change Your Life* (New York, NY: HarperCollins, 1999), 19.

Chapter 10:
Working With the Grain

1. Sonja Lyubomirsky, *The How of Happiness: A New Approach to Getting the Life You Want* (New York, NY: Penguin Press, 2008): 22.

2. Hara Estroff Marano, *A Nation of Wimps: The High Cost of Invasive Parenting* (New York, NY: Broadway Books, 2008), 229.

3. Ibid.

4. Ibid.

5. T. J. Mathews and Brady E. Hamilton, "Delayed Childbearing: More Women Are Having Their First Child Later in Life," *NCHS Data Brief* 21 (2009), accessed April 12, 2012, http://www.cdc.gov/nchs/data/databriefs/db21.pdf.

6. Rubén G. Rumbaut, "Young Adults in the United States: A Profile," *Research Network Working Paper No. 4* (2004): 6, accessed April 23, 2012, http://papers.ssrn.com/sol3/papers.cfm?abstract_id=1887827.

7. William S. Aquilino, "From Adolescent to Young Adult: A Prospective Study of Parent-Child Relations during the Transition to Adulthood," *Journal of Marriage and the Family* 59, no. 3 (1997): 682.

8. Laura A. King and Joshua A. Hicks, "Whatever Happened to 'What Might Have Been'? Regrets, Happiness and Maturity," *American Psychologist* 62, no. 7 (2007): 634.

9. King and Hicks, "Whatever Happened to 'What Might Have Been'?"; Varda Konstam, "Emerging Adults and Parental Divorce: Coming to Terms with 'What Might Have Been,'" *Journal of Systemic Therapies* 28, no. 4 (2009): 39.

10. Cynthia Broderick, "Top 10 Things to Do before You Turn 30," Bankrate.com, March 23, 2003, accessed February 3, 2012, http://www.bankrate.com/brm/news/advice/19990531a.asp.

11. John Zogby, *The Way We'll Be: The Zogby Report on the Transformation of the American Dream* (New York, NY: Random House, 2008), 197.

12. Anna Bahney, "A Life Between Jobs," *New York Times,* June 8, 2006, accessed December 14, 2011, http://www.nytimes.com/2006/06/08/fashion/thursdaystyles/08vaca.html?pagewanted=all.

13. Zogby, *The Way We'll Be,* 199.

14. Sharon Jayson, "Many 'Emerging Adults' 18–29 Are Not There Yet," *USA Today,* July 30, 2012, accessed August 15, 2012, http://usatoday30.usatoday.com/news/health/wellness/story/2012-07-30/Emerging-adults-18-29-still-attached-to-parents/56575404/1.

15. Jean M. Twenge, *Generation Me: Why Today's Young Americans are More Confident, Assertive, Entitled— and More Miserable Than Ever Before* (New York, NY: Free Press, 2006), 106–116.

16. Judith Warner, *Perfect Madness: Motherhood in the Age of Anxiety* (New York, NY: Riverhead Books, 2005), 163.

17. Lyubomirsky, *The How of Happiness,* 22–23.

18. Ibid.

19. Marianne Jacobbi, "You, Only Different: Why Do Girlfriends and Wives Keep Trying to Change Their Men," *The Boston Globe,* March 15, 2009, accessed November 4, 2011, http://www.boston.com/bostonglobe/magazine/articles/2009/03/15/you_only_different/.